BUSINESS LAW

ALISON PETERSON V. GROCERY DEPOT, INC.

MOCK TRIAL

Additional information and resources at www.bizlawbooks.com
For comments and questions email info@bizlawbooks.com

© 2013 Biz Law Books, LLC

All rights reserved. Copyright under Biz Law Books, LLC. No part of this book may be used or reproduced in any manner whatsoever without written permission of the Publisher.

Alison Peterson v. Grocery Depot, Inc.
Mock Trial

Jacket, interior design, and typography by Cameron Sandage

FOURTH EDITION

0 9 8 7 6 5 4 3 2 1

ISBN: 978-0-9786307-5-1

Printed in the United States of America

TABLE OF CONTENTS

FORWARD	4
WORKSHEET	6
INTRODUCTION	8
THE INCIDENT	**11**
Witness List	12
Complaint for Relief	13
Answer and Affirmative Defense	15
Plaintiff Witness: Deposition of Alison Petersonon	17
Plaintiff Witness: Statement of Douglas Saterson, M.D.	21
Plaintiff Witness: Statement of Marty Langner	22
Plaintiff Witness: Statement of Mika Drivesdale	23
Defense Witness: Statement of Tampica Hillstrom	25
Defense Witness: Statement of Debra Billings	27
Defense Witness: Expert Witness Barge County Safety Inspections	29
SUPPORTING RECORDS AND IMAGES	**35**
Incident Report Form From James D'Lake	36
Incident Report Form From Tampica Hillstrom	38
Barge County Paramedics Report	40
Barge County Hospital Emergency Room Report	42
Barge County Health Department Report	43
The Sunland Clinic	44
Grocery Depot Safety Policy	46
Grocery Depot Floor Plan	48
Department Of Corrections Arrest Record	49
Produce Department Floor Check Sheet	50
Deli Department Floor Check Sheet	52
Deli Receipt	54
Driver License	55
Visa	56
Banana Signage	57
STATE OF FOSTER STATUTES AND CASES	**61**
Statute And Case File	63
Foster Revised Statutes (FRS)	64
Jury Worksheet	66
Palsgraf Case	68
Palsgraf Case Worksheet	82
Overpeck Case	86
Overpeck Case Worksheet	94
Sullivan Case	98
Sullivan Case Worksheet	104
Elston Case	108
Elston Case Worksheet	126
SUPPORTING INFORMATION	**131**
Evidence Subject Tree	132
Evidence Outline	136
Tort Subject Tree	144
Tort Outline	146
Briefing A Legal Case	155
Motion In Limine	158
Rhythm Of A Trial	159
List Of Common Objections	160
GLOSSARY	**165**

ALISON PETERSON V. GROCERY DEPOT, INC.

The case has been set with the initial complaint and prayer for relief/damages, answer, witness statements, and evidentiary pieces that may be used by either side. The list of witness may be shortened if necessary to fit the class size or teaching preferences of the instructor; however, the witness list for the plaintiff and defense will be best utilized by starting from the top of each list. Ultimately, the plaintiff Alison Petersonon and the defendant James D'Lake (as representative of GDI) must at a minimum be used. Students should be organized into at least two teams of plaintiff and defense to fully perform this mock trial. However for the best results, the following organizational setup is suggested.

PLAINTIFF'S TEAM
- One student for each direct witness
- One student for each cross-examination witness
- One student for closing argument
- One student for each witness
- Often backups for each of the above are used for a team approach

DEFENSE'S TEAM
- One student for opening statement
- One student for each direct witness
- One student for each cross-examination witness
- One student for closing argument
- One student for each witness
- Often backups for each of the above are used for a team approach

OPTIONAL TEAMS IF YOUR CLASS SIZE PERMITS
- Three students to be a Judge panel that will hear all motions to the court and make decisions on evidence
- Two students to perform bailiff duties and aid in organization of the trial before and during trial
- 6-12 students to be on a jury and during preparation time may serve with other neutral duties
- Two students to be court clerks. These students would often aid in organizing the materials coming to the trial, what attorney will be questioning a witness and planning a timesheet for the trial to keep everyone on time

This mock trial works best when the students are studying personal injury in relation to a business environment. The facts of the case are set around a Negligence fact pattern with the elements of Duty of Care, Breach of that Duty,

FORWARD

Causation of both Proximate Cause / Actual Cause, and Damages. Any of the major defenses may be used or you may want to limit the defenses to those allowed in your jurisdiction.

Each student in the mock trial is given a role; however, the facts are intentionally left thin as to the actual character of the individual. This allows for each student to create the persona of the character as he/she sees fit and feels comfortable in the portrayal. By allowing the characters to become real to the student, the learning outcome is enhanced. As an added benefit to the instructor that may choose to teach this mock trial over-and-over again each time it is taught the outcome can be quite different and the characters portrayed can be different.

Even though the names of some of the parties in the case appear to be male or female, any character can be exchanged for another gender, as the outcome of the case is gender neutral.

Concerning the state of Foster, Barge County, city of Sunland, or any other names, cities, counties, states, addresses, all are created for this mock trial and are of no reference to a real place or jurisdiction. The facts of the case are fictional, but it should be noted that the facts are typical to thousands of real case facts and incidents.

Mistakes in this book. We are not perfect and no doubt there are some mistakes in this book. However, please note that in real cases the same mistakes and factual inaccuracies appear. The discrepancies in statements from witness to witness are not mistakes, but rather, these are a representation of different people seeing the facts of an incident from his/her own perspective. Even the same person may declare his/her facts/story differently after thinking about it over time; thus, this is one of the challenges with cases such as this type. Overall, this mock trial is not written in chronological order and one of the challenges for students is to go through the statements, evidences, complaint, and answer and try to put the puzzle together.

ALISON PETERSON V. GROCERY DEPOT, INC.

Note: An editable version of this worksheet may be obtained from the publisher by email info@BizLawBooks.com

A. Witness
B. Student(s) appointed to play part
C. Student(s) appointed from plaintiff's council for direct testimony and support
D. Student(s) appointed from defense's council for cross-examination testimony and support

PLANTIFF WITNESS

A	B	C	D
Alison Peterson	1. 2. 3.	1. 2. 3.	1. 2. 3.
Douglas Saterson, M.D.	1. 2. 3.	1. 2. 3.	1. 2. 3.
Marty Langner	1. 2. 3.	1. 2. 3.	1. 2. 3.
Mika Drivesdale	1. 2. 3.	1. 2. 3.	1. 2. 3.
Jacqueline Powell	1. 2. 3.	1. 2. 3.	1. 2. 3.
Rory Camichael, MD.	1. 2. 3.	1. 2. 3.	1. 2. 3.

WORKSHEET

DEFENSE WITNESSES

A	B	C	D
James D'Lake	1. 2. 3.	1. 2. 3.	1. 2. 3.
Tampica Hillstrom	1. 2. 3.	1. 2. 3.	1. 2. 3.
Debra Billings	1. 2. 3.	1. 2. 3.	1. 2. 3.
Erick Danner	1. 2. 3.	1. 2. 3.	1. 2. 3.
Irene Blessby, M.D.	1. 2. 3.	1. 2. 3.	1. 2. 3.
Hale Niles	1. 2. 3.	1. 2. 3.	1. 2. 3.
Paul Creat	1. 2. 3.	1. 2. 3.	1. 2. 3.

INTRODUCTION

"Slip and fall" cases are traditionally based on the duty of care that a possessor of land owes to an invitee. "A business visitor is a person who is invited to enter or remain on land for a purpose directly or indirectly connected with business dealings with the possessor of the land." Restatement (Second) of Torts § 332(3) (A.L.I.1965). A possessor of land is subject to liability for physical harm caused to his invitees by a condition on the land if... (See State of Foster Revised Statues in this textbook).

The Plaintiff in this case is alleging a slip and fall while shopping at Grocery Depot, Inc. (GDI). This case is factually complicated due to the differing opinions of eyewitness accounts as well as the facts told to us by the Plaintiff and Defendant. Prior to trial the parties have been able to stipulate to several facts that are listed below.

STIPULATED FACTS
1. Plaintiff was shopping in GDI on March 23, 2011.
2. Plaintiff's cousin, Mika Drivesdale purchased a soda drinks from the Deli Department at 1:05pm on March 23, 2011.
3. Plaintiff was discovered unconscious by Mika Drivesdale.
4. Incident occurred sometime between 1:50pm – 2:05pm
5. Tampica Hillstrom, Produce Department Manager, signed off having checked the floor at 1:20pm on March 23, 2011.
6. Debra Billings, Deli Clerk, signed off having checked the floor at 1:40pm
7. Plaintiff had partially smashed banana residue on her foot and there was smashed banana on the floor as well as some very light brown juice on the floor. Plaintiff had a bunch of three bananas in her cart.
8. GDI had overripe bananas on sale for 50 percent off regular price.
9. GDI's policy is to check the floor every 20 minutes for any problems.

THE INCIDENT

ALISON PETERSON V. GROCERY DEPOT, INC.

WITNESS LIST

PLAINTIFF WITNESSES
Alison Petersonon
Douglas Saterson, M.D.
Marty Langner, eyewitness of the incident. Customer at GDI.
Mika Drivesdale, Cousin to Alison Petersonon.
Jacqueline Powell, Health Inspector
Rory Carmichael, M.D. The Sunland Clinic

DEFENSE WITNESSES
James D'Lake, Grocery Depot, Inc. Store Manager
Tampica Hillstrom, Produce Department Manager
Debra Billings, Deli Clerk
Erick Danner, Safety Expert
Irene Blessby, M.D. serving as the emergency room doctor on staff.
Haley Niles, Paramedic
Paul Creat, Paramedic

THE INCIDENT

IN THE COURT OF BARGE COUNTY
STATE OF FOSTER CIVIL DIVISION

Alison Petersonon
    Plaintiff

v.   Docket # 11-0718-C

Grocery Depot, Inc.
    Defendant

COMPLAINT FOR RELIEF

I. Plaintifff Alison Petersonon is a resident of Barge County in the state of Foster and has resided here for the last 4 years. Alison Petersonon's address is 4823 NW Myrtle Avenue, Sunland, Foster 99586.

II. Defendant Grocery Depot, Inc. (GDI) is a corporation doing business here in Barge County, Foster at 15300 NE Dunes Boulevard, Sunland, Foster 99587. GDI's corporate office is located at this same address.

III. This court has jurisdiction over these matters as listed in the State of Foster Statutes Section 1-105, and venue is correct under Section 1-203.

IV. On March 23, 2011 Alison Petersonon and her cousin, Mika Drivesdale, were having lunch and shopping at GDI in the early afternoon for various grocery items, including produce.

V. Upon spending some time at the store, Alison Petersonon decided to look over the produce, and Mika Drivesdale decided to continue shopping on another aisle. The precise time of this is uncertain, but it can be narrowed down to entering the store at about 12:45pm, Alison and Mika having a soda together at 1:05pm and Alison being discovered on the floor at the corner of the Produce and Deli Department by 2:05pm.

VI. GDI was selling overripe bananas, which the bananas were stacked on a 4 foot square display measuring 36-inches from the floor. The bananas were marked "50% off Overripe Bananas, $0.99/Bunch (no separating of bunches)."

ALISON PETERSON V. GROCERY DEPOT, INC.

VII. Alison Petersonon had partially smashed banana residue on her foot and there was smashed banana on the floor as well as some very light brown juice on the floor in connection with the banana display.

VIII. Plaintiff alleges the floor of GDI was not properly maintained in a reasonable clean manner, nor was the part of the floor that was near such a volatile item that may leak checked often enough to cover GDI's duty of care to an invitee in its store.

Plaintiff alleges that GDI is culpable of NEGLIGENCE by not keeping its facility in a safe condition for invitees. Plaintif alleges a duty of care was owed and breached; GDI has a legal duty to act and therefore caused the injury.

THEREFORE, PLAINTIF PRAYS FOR THE FOLLOWING RELIEF:

I. All medical bills incurred due to this incident, which comprise of the following: $900.00
    A. Ambulance to Barge Country Emergeny Room $4,500.00
    Barge Country Emergency Room Treatment $12,000.00
    C. Barge Country Hospital stay for 4-nights $18,000.00
    D. Hip surgery $50,000.00
    E. Continued Medications for life
        $68,000.00

II. Compensatory damages for wages for two years
    $130,000.00

III. Attorney's fees and court cost
    $1,200,000.00

IV. Punitive damages
    $1,483,400.00

V. Total relief requested

Respectfully Submitted,

Paul Smitters

Paul Smitters
Paul Smitters, Attorney No. 97052
Smitters, Dane and Associates, PC
3726 NE Tenth Street, Suite 906 Sunland, Foster 99586
802.578.7456
Attorney for Plaintif

THE INCIDENT

IN THE COURT OF BARGE COUNTY
STATE OF FOSTER CIVIL DIVISION

Alison Petersonon
  Plaintiff

v. Docket # 11-0718-C

Grocery Depot, Inc.
  Defendant

ANSWER AND AFFIRMATIVE DEFENSE

I. Admitted

II. Admitted

III. Admitted

IV. Admitted

V. Admitted except for the time of discovery of Alison Petersonon on the floor at 2:05pm. We allege Alison must have been discovered not later than 1:50pm due to a floor inspection by Debra Billings, Deli Department Clerk.

VI. Admitted except for the part about the light brown juice in connection with the banana display. We allege this juice is in connection with Plaintiff's foot containing the smashed banana.

VII. Denied

VIII. Denied

AFFIRMATIVE DEFENSE

Grocery Depot, Inc. raises the following affirmative defense that any liquid found on the sales floor was caused by plaintiff by spilling her soda. Further, plaintiff caused herself to slip and fall when she dropped a banana and stepped on it.

ALISON PETERSON V. GROCERY DEPOT, INC.

THEREFORE, DEFENDANT PRAYS FOR THE FOLLOWING RELIEF:
Defendant has fully answered the complaint by plaintiff and believes there to be no prima facia case of negligence on the part of Grocery Depot, Inc and requests a dismissal in favor of Defendant. Defendant's prayer of relief is only that Plaintiff bear all court costs.

Respectfully Submitted,

Derrick Pathway

Derrick Pathway, Attorney No. 88131
Pathway & Pathway, PC
16101 NE Weldon Place, Suite 329 Sunland, Foster 99587
802.576.1065
Attorney for Defendant

THE INCIDENT

PLAINTIFF WITNESS
DEPOSITION OF ALISON PETERSONON
April 10, 2011

Q. Please state your full name, spell your last name, and state your address for the record please.

A. My name is Alison Petersonon, and I live at 4823 NW Myrtle Avenue Sunland, Foster 99586.

Q. How long have you lived at that address?

A. I have lived there for the past 4 years as my primary place of residence, but I do travel a lot and spend 2 to 3 months a year in Europe.

Q. How often do you shop at Grocery Depot when you are in town?

A. Well, I shop at a lot of stores for the best price because I don't have much money, so when the current advertisements come out, I plan to shop at GDI for all the things that are on sale each week.

Q. So, how often do you think that would be?

A. I shop at GDI each week about two or three times for little items because GDI is close to my home, but I usually shop one big time for most of my groceries.

Q. Concerning the events that occurred on March 23, 2011 at GDI, can you explain for me how you were feeling that day?

A. I was feeling fine. Well, I had a small headache and my knee ached earlier that day, but I am not young anymore. I would say that I was feeling fairly well by the time I went shopping later that day with my cousin.

Q. Have you had knee problems in the past?

A. Well, I have not ever needed surgery if that is what you mean. But, on occasion, my right knee aches and gives me trouble supporting my weight on bad days.

ALISON PETERSON V. GROCERY DEPOT, INC.

Q. How often do you have bad days?

A. Not very often, but I would guess about once per month lately. I usually take a break to sit when I am shopping and rest the knee so I do not stress it out.

Q. On March 23, you and your cousin took a break at the deli and purchased a soda. Were you taking a break for your knee at that time?

A. Oh, for heavens sakes no! I cannot travel anywhere with my cousin that she doesn't have to stop for a cold drink. So, we stopped and she drank a soda, and I bought one too, but I just sipped at it and took it with me when we left the deli to keep sipping on it.

Q. After you left the deli, where did you go?

A. I started shopping again. I was looking for raisins because the kids love to have those little boxes as a snack. I headed over near the produce department, which is next to the deli. But, I thought I would find raisins in the dried fruit section one aisle over, so I went down that aisle but did not see the raisins.

Q. Did you continue looking for the raisins?

A. Yes, I went over to the produce department to ask for help finding them, but that is when I saw the bananas for sale. When my cousin and I were sitting at the deli we could see bananas for sale, but I did not see the overripe special sale of 50 percent off. Well, you know I love a good deal because I am low income you know.

Q. So, what happened next after you saw the overripe bananas for sale?

A. Everything gets very fuzzy from this point because I was looking at the bananas and slipped on something on the floor and fell to the ground. Next thing I knew I was in the emergency room. I guess I had been knocked unconscious from that fall, which broke my hip and shattered my hip socket.

Q. I would like to talk about the events just prior to your fall. Can you tell me exactly what the banana sign said?

THE INCIDENT

A. I remember seeing "Overripe Bananas 50% off." I do not think it said anything else that was readable. Of course, I did not have my glasses on for reading and my vision is not perfect.

Q. Did you drive to the store that day?

A. Yes. I always like to drive my car. Besides, my cousin's car is too small for me.

Q. What happened to the soda drink you were carrying from the deli? And, I do not remember if you stated this, but what type of soda drink was it?

A. It was Grocery Depot brand cola, and I do not remember what happened to it, but I must have set it down in the deli.

Q. What kind of floor surface were you standing on in the overripe banana area?

A. I do not recall other than a tile floor, but periodically throughout the produce area there are rubber mats and some small carpet pieces to keep people from falling, but I do not remember anything like that where I was standing.

Q. How are you feeling today with regard to your injury?

A. I am getting much better. I can actually get out of bed by myself now, but the doctor said my hip would not be 100 percent for a long time if ever.

Q. Is there anything else you would like to say?

A. Yes, I have been shopping at this store the entire time I have lived here, and it has always been a mess. I only come here for the good prices because I am low income. The store never seems to have enough employees to help the customers, and on many occasions I have left the building because the store was out of the advertised item! I reported the store to the health department one year ago (see health department report), but I was told that GDI had a score of 96 percent. I do not believe the health department even looked into the problem. Also, all of the shopping carts I have used are terrible, and I remember the cart I was pushing had a bad wheel on the back. The cart pulled to the right as I pushed it, and I had to pay close attention to insure the cart was still squarely in front of me because when I am shopping, I am busy looking at stuff and not at my cart all the time. It is just another unsafe thing that GDI is doing and refuses to fix! Me and Mika just get our bargains and get out of there.

THE INCIDENT

PLAINTIFF WITNESS
STATEMENT OF DOUGLAS SATERSON, M.D.
March 29, 2011

I was not the initial treating physician when Alison Petersonon arrived at the emergency room of Barge County Hospital, but I was paged to come and see an emergency patient (Alison Petersonon) due to the complications of the injury. I arrived at 3:10pm, and Alison was awake and complaining of a lot of pain in her hip, lower back, knee, and radiating down to her ankle and foot on her right side.

At the initial arrival, Alison was unable to fully respond to my questions in a coherent manner, and she had much ramblings resulting in non-sensible murmurs that were never interpreted by anyone to my knowledge. Alison's cousin, Mika Drivesdale, was at Alison's side and appeared very knowledgeable about Alison's health. We administered pain medication and began calling to find someone that could make health decisions, but by the time we reached her husband, Alison regained enough capacity to have a conversation.

Alison told me that she had fallen at Grocery Depot, Inc. and could not remember how she had gotten to the hospital. Alison's last memory was standing at the banana display. I asked Alison about her overall health. She said her knee has been hurting for years and seems to be affecting her whole right side.

Upon examination with full X-rays and MRI for soft tissue damage, I diagnosed Alison with a broken hipbone cracked all the way into the socket; the hip socket is fractured all the way around showing signs of much trauma. Alison's knee is shifted to the right and appears to have worn into that position for some time. This fall has further pushed the knee to the right complicating the problem, which should result in a knee replacement.

Alison will need hip surgery and knee replacement surgery. Her recovery is not expected to be 100 percent. Alison's health was not 100 percent prior to this incident, which plays a large factor in recovery. Alison should be able to recover 80 to 85 percent use in both the hip and knee with successful surgeries along with a minimum one year of rehabilitation.

ALISON PETERSON V. GROCERY DEPOT, INC.

PLAINTIFF WITNESS
STATEMENT OF MARTY LANGNER, EYEWITNESS OF THE INCIDENT
March 23, 2011

My name is Marty Langner. I am 73 years old and a regular shopper at Grocery Depot, Inc. My address is as follows:

874 SW Maple Avenue Sunland, Foster 99567

I was shopping at the Grocery Depot on March 23, 2011 at the time Alison fell. I was on the other side of the display from where she was, which is where the regular bananas are located. Alison caught my eye because she had one of those bad shopping carts that kept thumping along and it appeared to make her walk funny with a kind of limp. Anyway, I was trying to pick a good ripe banana, and I had wanted to purchase one of those overripe bananas, but the sign said not to divide the bunches, and the smallest bunch I could find had five bananas.

When I walked away from the display, Alison was still looking through the bananas. I went over to the watermelons and looked up just in time to see Alison go down to the floor, but I thought she bent down to the floor to pick up something, so I did not hurry over to her. I continued shopping for a bit. I have tried to remember how much time passed, but I tend to lose track of time, but I think it was about two minutes. I walked over to take a look at the peaches, and her cousin Mika Drivesdale was treating her on the floor. Alison appeared to be unconscious. I was standing with Alison's feet pointed toward me, and there was some brown liquid on the floor. The liquid was a very small amount – maybe enough for a tablespoon or two.

I noticed a part of a banana smashed on the floor. I had noticed when I was looking at the overripe bananas that some of the bananas in the display on the bottom were getting smashed and saucy. I wondered if one of those smashed bananas clung to a bunch Alison had picked up. The smashed banana could have fallen to the floor, but those are just my thoughts.

It is too bad that Alison did not land on the rubber mat that was on one side of the overripe banana display because it could have helped break her fall or helped her to not slip at all.

THE INCIDENT

PLAINTIFF WITNESS
STATEMENT OF MIKA DRIVESDALE, COUSIN TO ALISON PETERSON
April 12, 2011

My name is Mika Drivesdale, and I live at 3787 NW Barnacle Street, Sunland, Foster 99586, which is just down the road from my cousin Alison Petersonon. I was shopping with Alison (I call her Ali) on the day of the accident. Ali and I shop together a lot, and Ali likes to go to Grocery Depot, but I don't care for it because it is a disgusting place to shop. Grocery Depot has great sales, so we go to get the sale items, but then I want to get out of there. Ali and I are very close, and Ali is a wonderful, caring, and loving person that would not ever hurt anybody. I am a couple years younger than Ali, and we have been best of friends all our lives.

That day, March 23rd, we took off that morning to go shopping at several stores, and Grocery Depot was third or fourth on our list. If the accident had not happened, we had a couple more stores to go to for sale items. When we shop, I try to do a lot of the running for stuff so that Ali does not have to do any extra walking because her knee is just not very good anymore. We started shopping at Grocery Depot right after coming across the street from another store, so we had been walking for a while. I decided to buy both of us sodas in the deli department so we could rest for a while.

Our friend, Debra Billings, was working in the deli that day, and she came out and sat down with us. Debra is great and sometimes gives us a discount on items even when I do not think they are on sale. We sat and talked with Debra for quite a while when the store manager came by and acted annoyed that Debra was taking a break. I am not surprised because this is not a good place to work according to Debra and from what I can see.

After leaving the deli, Ali was looking for raisins, and I went across the store looking for molasses and brown sugar for some cookies that Ali and I were going to make later. These items were on the baking aisle about seven or eight aisles away, but I knew right where to find them. When I came back to look for Ali, I went to the produce department where the raisins are located. I did a quick scan for Ali and did not see her, so I called out for her, but she did not answer. It was right then I saw her on the ground. I screamed, "Ali! Somebody come help!" Ali was next to the overripe banana display between the produce and deli departments, and she was unconscious.

ALISON PETERSON V. GROCERY DEPOT, INC.

Tampica Hillstrom was the first employee on the scene, and she told somebody to get an ambulance, but I was screaming at Tampica, "Call 911!" Tampica is an idiot. Debra used to work with her, and Tampica did not ever treat Debra very well, and in fact Tampica used to make Debra do all the clean-up work while Tampica got to do all the creating of displays and fun stuff. Anyway, an ambulance did finally arrive and took Ali to the hospital.

I was amazed that I was the first on the scene because Ali must have been laying there for several minutes. Grocery Depot is so short staffed they do not even check for people that have fallen down. The store manager came running down to see what happened, and Tampica started telling him a bunch of lies that Ali must have "passed out or maybe she had a seizure." The problem was obviously right in front of us all. "Nobody checked the floor! The overripe bananas leaked and had fallen onto the floor."

After the ambulance had gone, I heard Tampica talking with the store manager, James D'Lake, and James said, "I think this is the same old crazy lady that tried to get us in trouble with the Health Department." I heard Tampica respond, "Yes, I think that is right, and we need to be careful because they are friends with Debra. I hope this is not charged to my department because it will affect my bonus." I told James to leave everything the way it was until I could get a camera and take a picture, and he said he would leave it. I went to the front of the store and bought a camera, but when I came back, everything was cleaned up and our shopping cart was gone. Stupid store manager! James claimed to know nothing of this cleanup, but I think he knows that the store is in trouble, and he made sure it was cleaned up as fast as possible. I will never shop at this store again.

From what I can remember, there was not any rubber mat or carpet near the overripe bananas, and the display was very sloppy. I know Ali did want some overripe bananas because we had looked at another store for some, but they were all green. She wanted to make some banana pudding, but the bananas must be really ripe or it turns out sour.

THE INCIDENT

DEFENSE WITNESS
STATEMENT OF TAMPICA HILLSTROM, PRODUCE DEPT. MANAGER
March 23, 2011

My name is Tampica Hillstrom, and I manage the Produce Department at Grocery Depot, Inc. I have worked for GDI for the past five years in several departments. I was in the back room of the Produce Department trimming lettuce when I heard the scream for help from Mika Drivesdale. I ran out to the floor to find Alison Petersonon unconscious on the floor. I asked if she was breathing because I know CPR, and I was told that she was breathing. I shouted to a customer to call 911, but instead of calling 911 the customer said the ambulance station was just next door to the store and he ran over to get it. Anyway, somehow the paramedics arrived and started working on Alison. In the meantime, I called my store manager, James D'Lake, and he arrived within one minute of getting the message.

I have seen Alison in the store for years, and she always appears to be limping and struggling along. A few months ago Alison was asking me when the watermelons would begin to arrive, and I told her I would go and check with the warehouse. Alison asked if I would come and find her in the deli after I got the information because she needed to sit down due to her knee problem. I got the information for her and found her sitting in the deli as she had said.

I noticed there was some brown liquid on the floor near Alison's foot, but it did not look like syrup from the banana display, although there was a smashed banana on Alison's foot. There were not any spills or bananas on the floor when I had one of my produce employees check the floor just a little while ago. I am very careful about stuff like this, and, in fact, I put down a rubber mat on the front side of the display and faced the sign towards the front. The sign could also be read from the back of the display, so I put a carpet down. Each department keeps a record of when we check the floor for spills, and as the manager I make a rule that we check the floor on the top of the hour, 20 minutes after the hour, and 40 minutes after the hour. This is, of course, in addition to our general alertness to conditions as we are working on the floor.

ALISON PETERSON V. GROCERY DEPOT, INC.

On the Overripe Banana sign I put "50% off Overripe Bananas, $0.99/Bunch (no separating of bunches)" (see banana sign). I noticed the sign had been partly turned to face the side of the display, and there was a spilled soda drink near the base of the display. I saw Alison sitting at the deli sipping a soda with her cousin, Mika Drivesdale, and I went over and said hello. I noticed Debra Billings (deli clerk) was sitting with them talking, and I thought that was odd, but I am not surprised as Debra is not a dedicated worker and I do not want her in my department. Debra used to be in my department, but I requested her to be transferred to another department because she is sloppy with her work, non-caring, and shows no sense of urgency in getting her job done.

I always try to make contact with our regular customers, although Alison is a bit of a troublemaker in our store. I understand that she was responsible for reporting us to the health department on some trumped-up charge that was later dismissed. I hope Alison does not come back to shop at our store as she is not a good customer and neither is her horrible, mouthy cousin Mika.

I also noticed Alison had a freshly separated bunch of bananas in her cart, and I think the one on the floor may have been separated from that bunch. Our sign said NO separating of bunches. This is typical for Alison and Mika as they always want a special deal or special treatment.

THE INCIDENT

DEFENSE WITNESS
STATEMENT OF DEBRA BILLINGS, DELI CLEARK GROCERY DEPOT, INC.
March 23, 2011

My name is Debra Billings, and I work at Grocery Depot, Inc. as a Deli Clerk. I have worked at GDI for about five months as a part-time employee while I am finishing college.

I was the one that signed the log stating I checked the floor at 1:40pm. Our deli manager says we must check the floor three times per hour: top of the hour, twenty minutes after the hour, and forty minutes after the hour. I know that the store policy says to check three times per hour. I am a friend to most of the workers in the store. We check the floor as much as possible and just sign showing the floor check was done on the designated time. In reality, the sales floor is checked as often as we have time, but not exactly when the manager says to check it, but I do not argue about it; instead, I just sign in the next spot.

We are way understaffed and everyone hates the store manager here at GDI. This is just a transition job for most people. The store is making lots of money, and they do not pay us hardly enough to pay rent in the slum area here in Sunland. I am not surprised Alison had an accident because the produce department is always a mess. I used to work in the produce department, but I asked for a transfer to the deli because Tampica Hillstrom, produce manager, was horrible to work for. I am amazed people will shop in that department because it is so messy and unkempt.

I served Alison Petersonon and her cousin, Mika, their sodas on the day of the accident. Alison and I have become good friends, and she has invited me to her house on several occasions. Alison is always looking for a good deal and she loves to shop our advertised products because GDI runs really hot deals to get customers in the door. I tell Alison in advance if I know of an advertised item that is coming up.

About one month ago Mika was not available, so Alison called me at home and asked if I could drive her to a doctor appointment. I was glad to do it. Alison told me she was having a lot of knee pain, and that it had collapsed the day before the appointment. However, she seemed to be able to walk quite well going to the appointment.

ALISON PETERSON V. GROCERY DEPOT, INC.

On the day of the accident, Mika was driving everyone crazy with her constant loud talking in the store. Mika said she talks loud so Alison can hear her, but I have not noticed any problem with Alison's hearing. I think Mika just wants to talk loud and be obnoxious. Anyway, the store manager came through the department in a big hurry while I was talking with Alison and Mika and asked me what I was doing. I was sitting with my friends, and I told him I was on break now.

After Alison fell down, Mika went crazy. I went over and talked with her for about a half hour to calm her down. I finally got her calmed down, and I was planning to drive her to the hospital, but Mika had to find another way of getting there because we were so short-handed in the deli I could not leave. Later that day, I went to see Alison in the hospital and she did not look good, but I was happy to see she was conscious and doing better.

THE INCIDENT

DEFENSE WITNESS – EXPERT WITNESS
BARGE COUNTY SAFETY INSPECTIONS, LLC
April 17, 2011

Inspector Name Erick Danner, Health and Safety Expert

BACKGROUND
1992 - Bachelor of Science University of Michigan
     Major: Engineering, Social Sciences
1995 - Master of Workplace Health and Safety, University of Washington
2001 - Ph.D. in Safety Engineering in the Workplace, Duke University
2001 - Barge County Safety Inspection Certificate
1992 - 2000 worked for Boeing Corporation as Workplace Health & Safety Advisor Manager
2000 - Currently own and operate Barge County Safety Inspections, LLC.

Barge County Safety Inspections, LLC is a privately owned company by Erick Danner. Currently, we hire nine full-time certified inspectors. We are licensed and able to inspect for Barge County when the county has overflow work, which seems to occur several times per year. Most of our business is private inspections to improve the working conditions for workers in a company. We also do private inspections and testify to our results in court as a hired expert witness.

Here we have been hired to do a full business inspection of Grocery Depot, Inc. We requested to not know the issues of concern in advance in order to maintain a non-biased report. Below are the findings of the comprehensive inspection of the working conditions and customer conditions at Grocery Depot, Inc. located at 15300 NE Dunes Boulevard, Sunland, Foster 99587.

CRITICAL CONCERNS
1. Rodent droppings found around inside perimeter of entire store.
2. Cracked glass on six of the upright freezer doors.
3. Many flies around the produce department due to too much overripe produce.

GENERAL CONCERNS
1. Trash bins in back of store are unsecured, which allows for rodent infestations.
2. Parking lot is cluttered with trash and is a hazard to both customers and employees.

ALISON PETERSON V. GROCERY DEPOT, INC.

3. Business entranceway on both sides does not give enough free clearance inside the building for customers to manage their groceries.
4. General clutter around store, but not significant to result in safety issue. It is, however, a distraction to a productive working environment.
5. Broken carts. About half of the shopping carts have some sort of major problem.
6. Store lighting is poor due to 20 percent of the lights not working.
7. Break room refrigerator needs a thorough cleaning.
8. Break room microwave is broken and should be discarded.
9. General aisles in the store have far too many floor stacked inventory items making it difficult to navigate for the customer and worker.
10. Bathrooms are cluttered with many problems including broken mirror, no toilet paper holder, sink tilted to the left, and paper towel dispenser not functioning (but paper towels were available).

AREAS OF EXCELLENCE
1. Check-stands are clean and have a free workflow.
2. Employee demeanor is happy, cheerful, and motivated.
3. Meat department is the high point of the store – sparkling.

This report is not intended to make note of all normal issues; rather, we have made note of Critical and General areas of concern as well as a few areas of Excellence. The areas of the store not mentioned in this report fall somewhere between General areas of concern and Areas of Excellence.

Report Respectfully Submitted,

Erick Danner, PhD.

Erick Danner, Ph.D. Health and Safety Expert
11484 NE Hippopotamus Place Sunland, Foster 99587
802.578.3199

THE INCIDENT

ALISON PETERSON V. GROCERY DEPOT, INC.

THE INCIDENT

SUPPORTING RECORDS, REPORTS AND IMAGES

ALISON PETERSON V. GROCERY DEPOT, INC.

GROCERY DEPOT, INC. INCIDENT REPORT FORM

This form is to be completed and submitted to our insurance carrier by the area manager and store manager on the day of the incident.

DATE: March 23, 2011
TIME: 3:30pm
REPORTED BY: James D'Lake, Grocery Depot, Inc. Store Manager

DESCRIBE THE INCIDENT WITH AS MUCH DETAIL AS POSSIBLE

My name is James D'Lake and I have been the Store Manager for the past six years at Grocery Depot, Inc. located at 15300 NE Dunes Boulevard, Sunland, Foster 99587. I am quite proud of my store and all the workers as we are supplying a great value to the community of low-cost groceries. In order to do this, we maintain a no-frills store with staffing that is highly motivated to getting a job done in an efficient manner consistently. This allows us to offer great prices to the community.

I was at the store on March 23, 2011 when the incident occurred. I have seen Alison in our store many times and she is a wonderful customer. Earlier that day, I saw Debra Billings (deli clerk) sitting with Alison and Mika, which surprised me because Debra is not allowed to take her break on the sales floor, but I did not say anything to her in front of the customers.

I was in my office when I got the call at about 2pm that a customer had fallen down. Well, of course I ran down to find out what happened and learned that an ambulance had already been called by Tampica Hillstrom, Produce Department manager, which makes me proud to see my staff working so hard to help.

UPON ARRIVAL I TOOK NOTE OF THE FOLLOWING THINGS:

- Alison Petersonon was on the floor and I was told she was unconscious. There was a smashed banana on Alison's foot.

- The location of the incident was right between the Produce and Deli departments located at the end of the produce just as you are entering the deli.

- There was a light brown liquid on the floor near Alison's foot.

- Alison was not standing on the front side of the display on the rubber mat or on the direct back of the display on the carpet; rather, Alison was on the side of the display.

- There was a spilled soft drink in the overripe bananas.

- The "Overripe Banana" sign had been turned a quarter turn to be read from the side, and the spilled soft drink cup was near the base of the sign.

Overall, the floor was very clean for the middle of the day and the large amount of customer flow that we have during this time. Tampica Hillstrom did a great job by putting the overripe bananas into a display that has a flat bottom to eliminate such problems of leaking. It did not appear that the leak came from the bananas but from the spilled soda drink. Leaking bananas are usually sticky and do not usually make juice that could run down the side of a display and pool on the floor

Later, Tampica Hillstrom said that Alison had a partial bunch of bananas in her cart, which our sign said to NOT separate the bunches. I went back to take a look in her cart, but the cart was gone with no trace of it to my knowledge. I believe my wonderful staff just put the items back on the shelf and cleaned the mess up once the ambulance had taken Alison away because we had a lot of customers to serve. As our store policy states, "Clean up spills promptly. Check the floor for any problems every 20 minutes within your own department." This is a policy that I strictly enforce and the staff does a great job.

ALISON PETERSON V. GROCERY DEPOT, INC.

GROCERY DEPOT, INC. INCIDENT REPORT FORM

This form is to be completed and submitted to our insurance carrier by the area manager and store manager on the day of the incident.

DATE: March 23, 2011
TIME: 3:30pm
REPORTED BY: Tampica Hillstrom, Produce Department Manager

DESCRIBE THE INCIDENT WITH AS MUCH DETAIL AS POSSIBLE

At approximately 1:50pm on March 23, 2011 a customer, Alison Petersonon, fell while passing between the produce and deli departments. Possibly, Alison was looking at the overripe banana display when she fell and was found unconscious. Her cousin, Mika Drivesdale, and I found her at about the same time, but Mika was there a moment before me. I notified the store manager, James D'Lake promptly, and he arrived on the scene within one minute. Alison was not revived to consciousness in the store, but I understand that she was revived to consciousness soon after being taken away in the ambulance.

There was a brown liquid on the floor that appeared to be cola soda. The cola soda was all on the side of the display and not directly in the front where the sign was supposed to be facing (the sign had been slightly turned). In Alison's cart was a bunch of bananas freshly separated at the stem, which the sign for the overripe bananas clearly read to NOT separate any bunches. The bananas were marked 50 percent off. I was trying to get rid of this inventory because it was not going to last another day.

Before the paramedics arrived, Mika was screaming and completely out of control. I thought the paramedics would have to settle her down. There was a smashed banana under Alison's foot, but I think that occurred after she had fallen.

As noted on the floor inspection report, the floor has been regularly checked for hazards by both the produce and deli departments.

SUPPORTING RECORDS, REPORTS AND IMAGES

ALISON PETERSON V. GROCERY DEPOT, INC.

BARGE COUNTY PARAMEDICS REPORT
March 23, 2011
Time Admited: 2:35 pm

Paramedics serving this call:
- Haley Niles
- Paul Creat

Arrived on scene at 2:19 pm
Patient Name Alison Petersonon
Date of Birth 9-12-1948

SUBJECTIVE OBSERVATIONS
- Cousin Mika Drivesdale was shouting upon our arrival that Ali (the patient) was dead and was creating a commotion
- Paul Creat had to take time to calm Mika down so that I/Haley could begin work on patient
- GDI workers were busy in the area with mops and attempting to create some order

OBJECTIVE OBSERVATIONS
- Trip was slightly delayed due to weather and traffic
- Alison laying mostly on right side
- Patient unresponsive to oral commands
- Patient was breathing well and was revived with smelling salts
- Patient had trouble regaining full comprehension for several minutes
- Asked patient if she was on any medications and she stated she was but could not relate what the medication were or when they were last taken
- Patient is complaining of extreme pain to her right hip, right shoulder, right ankle
- Patient had a large bump on back right side of her head but she did not mention it as a complaint
- Patient appears to have some old bruising on the upper thigh area as observed by a yellowing coloration
- Vitals
 - Blood pressure: 147/105
 - Pulse: 115 bpm
 - Right and Left Eyes: dilated
 - Temperature: Unknown

ASSESSMENT OF THE SITUATION
- Patient appeared stable
- Patient appears to be in a lot of pain

PLAN OF ACTION
- Transport patient to hospital
- Keep patient as calm as possible
- Attempt to learn of medications while in transit to aid emergency room with information

ALISON PETERSON V. GROCERY DEPOT, INC.

BARGE COUNTY HOSPITAL EMERGENCY ROOM REPORT
March 23, 2011
Time Admitted 2:35pm.

Report created by Irene Blessby, M.D. serving as the emergency room doctor on staff.

Patient Name: Alison Petersonon   DOB 9-12-1948
Foster I.D.   QN-672183
Height 5 feet, 6 inches   Weight 217 pounds
Medication currently being taken:
Vicodin 500mg twice/day for knee pain. Prescribing Dr. Rory Carmichael, M.D.
- Patient says she only takes this about once per week

Alison Petersonon had apparently fallen at Grocery Depot, Inc. where the paramedics picked her off of the ground and transported her to Barge County Hospital. Alison arrived in an unconscious state at 2:35pm, but she was promptly revived to minimal conscious levels with the use of smelling salts.

After a general evaluation, Alison was rushed in for X-rays for an apparent broken hip and knee problems resulting from the fall. Dr. Douglas Saterson, Bone and Joint Specialist, was called immediately.

Upon arrival, Alison had smashed banana residue on the sole of her right foot. She was wearing sweat pants, a loose fitting top, and white tennis shoes.

During X-rays Alison constantly complained of much pain. The emergency room doctor noted the following issues as a general observation to Alison's physical appearance, demeanor, and palpation tests:
  Cannot bend knee without pain
  Cannot sit up without screaming in pain
  Has bruises in the following areas:
  - Back of head
  - Right shoulder
  - Right elbow
  - Hip area in general

Does not have any marks of bruising around the knee, but the knee is hot and swelling a bit.

Further tests and a final diagnosis are being conducted by Douglas Saterson, M.D. Bone and Joint Specialist.

SUPPORTING RECORDS, REPORTS AND IMAGES

BARGE COUNTY HEALTH DEPARTMENT REPORT
February 16, 2010
Intake Health Inspector Jacqueline Powell

CITIZEN COMPLAINT
NAME: Alison Petersonon
ADDRESS: 4823 NW Myrtle Avenue, Sunland, Foster 99586.
PHONE: 802.578.4578

COMPLAINT DETAILS
Grocery Depot, Inc. located at 15300 NE Dunes Boulevard, Sunland, Foster 99587. The store is dirty with actual spills on the floors that are not cleaned for more than an hour at a time. Meat is not kept under reasonable refrigeration. Cartons of eggs are sitting on the floor and not in refrigeration. Rodent holes and tracks can be seen under the produce counters, and there was at least one episode that a rat was seen running along the edge of the wall in the back room, which was seen when Alison had to use the restroom.

FINDINGS
I made a full inspection of Grocery Depot, Inc. one month prior to this complaint on January 12, 2010, and I found minor code issues as follows:
1. Flies near the produce area due to rotting fruit
2. Refrigeration one degree too warm in one section of the poultry meat
3. Ants in the back room

I rescheduled for another inspection in two weeks and gave GDI an initial score of 76 percent which any score below 80 percent puts the facility on automatic probation for six months. One week later I was supplied by facsimile a report by Quick Extermination, LLC. The report stated the fly and ant problem at GDI and how it was fully corrected. Further, I was supplied by facsimile a report by Freezers-R-US, LLC. This report stated the repair of the refrigeration and cited temperatures that had been taken over a six hour period all within code. With all this work being done so rapidly, I called the store manager and commended his diligence. I rescored the facility at 96 percent and sent the certificate by fax. Finally, I cancelled the re-inspection. Since the report had not been entered into the permanent record, I was able to rescind it and issue the new report.

With these concerns in mind, I went to GDI on February 17, 2010 at 9:00am. I found no support for any of the claims asserted by the Citizen Complaint, and I found the store in excellent condition health wise. File closed and marked as an Unsubstantiated Complaint. No further action necessary.

ALISON PETERSON V. GROCERY DEPOT, INC.

The Sunland Clinic
"Wellness and Healing is Our Focus"
1739 S. Main St. Sunland, Foster 99587

May 4, 2011

Primary Care Physician: Rory Carmichael
Patient: Alison Petersonon

Alison Petersonon has been under my care for the last 16-months. I have seen Alison 4 times for regular appointments, and I continue to treat Alison for her health conditions. One condition that Alison initially complained about was her knee pain, which I have reached no long-term conclusions as to her health plan for full recovery at this time. I am treating her pain issues and monitoring the knee to become stable. Some of Alison's health problems are due to her weight and I am working with Alison on a plan to lower her weight and take strain from her knee joint.

I have written a prescription for some pain medication, which can be seen as an attachment to this file. The prescription was written on March 14, 2011 and my office was notified that it was filled on March 16, 2011. Alison has described her pain 16-months ago as a level 7 on a scale of 1-10 with 1 being low pain and 10 being extreme pain. She complained that her knee would ache so much at night that she could hardly sleep and that her sleeplessness was hurting her quality of life and making her dizzy in the daytime.

Additionally, I have written a letter and filled out an application for Alison to acquire a disabled parking permit when she first came to see me as a patient. This was done to limit how far she has to walk in an uncontrolled environment. While exercise is clearly part of the overall program I am working with Alison on, exercise needs to be in a controlled environment that will allow her to maximize her health benefits and minimize her risk of harm to herself. I have no knowledge whether Alison acquired or uses the parking permit.

RORY CARMICHAEL, M.D.
1739 S. MAIN ST.
SUNLAND, FOSTER 99587

Vicodin 500 mg
sig 1-2 pills every 6 hours as needed for pain
qty 20 / Refills x3

DATE April 14, 2011   RoryCarmichael **M.D.**

ALISON PETERSON V. GROCERY DEPOT, INC.

GROCERY DEPOT, INC. SAFETY POLICY
SECTION 1

1. GENERAL SAFETY CHECKLIST
This is a general list of both areas of concern for each employee to watch and basic guidelines. Every employee has a responsibility to look for possible hazards. If hazard or condition is spotted, report it to your supervisor immediately.

1.1. All breaks are to be taken in the designated break room.

1.2. All lunch breaks are to be taken in the designated break room or off of the GDI's property (does not include sitting in your car).

1.3. Assist customers in lifting and loading heavy items.

1.4. Blocked aisles.

1.5. Blocked fire doors.

1.6. Blocked fire extinguishers, hose sprinkler heads.

1.7. Clean up spills promptly. Check the floor for any problems every 20 minutes. within your own department.

1.8. Dangerously piled supplies or equipment.

1.9. Directional or warning signs not in place.

1.10. Each department must keep a signed log as to when the floor was checked.

1.11. Electrical equipment left operating.

1.12. Evidence of any equipment running hot or overheating.

1.13. Evidence of smoking in non-smoking areas.

1.14. Good common sense as a member of this store community is mandated.

SUPPORTING RECORDS, REPORTS AND IMAGES

1.15. Leaks of steam, water, oil, etc.

1.16. Loose handrails or guard rails.

1.17. Loose or broken windows.

1.17.1. Machine, power transmission, or drive guards missing, damaged, loose, or improperly placed.

1.18. Maintain a professional appearance at all times.

1.19. Missing (or inoperative) entrance/exit signs and lighting.

1.20. Open doors on electrical panels.

1.21. Open or broken windows.

1.22. Poorly lighted stairs, walkways or areas.

1.23. Roof leaks.

1.24. Safety devices not operating properly.

1.25. Slippery floors and walkways.

1.26. Tripping hazards, such as rugs, mats, inventory on floor, etc.

2. INJURED PERSONS
2.1. Report to store manager immediately.

2.2. Do not move injured party until it is safe to do so.

2.3. Call for emergency assistance promptly by calling 911.

2.4. Call for at least two other employees to help evaluate the situation.

These safety guidelines are not to be viewed as a comprehensive list, but rather as a guideline. Every employee of Grocery Depot, Inc. should use common sense and good judgment at all times.

ALISON PETERSON V. GROCERY DEPOT, INC.

GROCERY DEPOT FLOOR PLAN

Alison Peterson was found at the X.

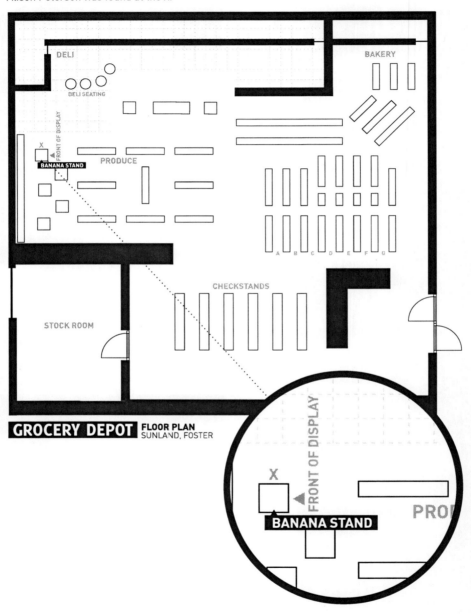

SUPPORTING RECORDS, REPORTS AND IMAGES

STATE OF FOSTER
DEPARTMENT OF CORRECTIONS ARREST RECORD

Name Alison Petersonon
Foster I.D. QN-672183
DOB 09-12-1948

DATE	CITY, STATE	RECORD #	OFFENSE	DISPOSITION
2/3/1962	Tampa, Florida	#B625492	Minor in Possession of Alcohol	GUILTY. One year probation, and attend alcohol abuse class.
7/4/1971	Washington, D.C.	#GYM3871	Counterfeiting and Conveyance of Counterfeited money	GUILTY. Eighteen months federal prison. Three years probation.
11/24/2003	Portland, Oregon	#KZ32263	DUII	DISMISSED
12/27/2004	Lake Oswego, Oregon	#L54492	Larceny	GUILTY. Six months jail. One year probation.
5/21/2009	Sunland, Foster	#E782191	Credit Card Fraud and Identity Theft	GUILTY. Five years probation.

ALISON PETERSON V. GROCERY DEPOT, INC.

PRODUCE DEPEARTMENT FLOOR CHECK REPORT

To all produce department employees.

Three times per hour the produce and deli department floor areas must be inspected for spills, dirt, or any other hazards that may need attention. Someone from the produce department must sign the form below indicating the floor has been inspected. Further, always remain aware of problems that may arise on an on going basis.

March 23, 2011

TIME	PLACE "X" IF INSPECTED	INITIALS
6:00 AM	x	KI
6:20 AM	x	KI
6:40 AM	x	KI
7:00 AM	x	KI
7:20 AM	x	KI
7:40 AM	x	KI
8:00 AM	x	KI
8:20 AM	x	KI
8:40 AM		
9:00 AM	X	
9:20 AM	X	PK
9:40 AM	X	PK
10:00 AM	X	PK
10:20 AM	X	PK
10:40 AM	x	TH
11:00 AM	x	
11:20 AM	x	TH
11:40 AM	x	TH
12:00 PM	x	TH
12:20 PM	x	TH

SUPPORTING RECORDS, REPORTS AND IMAGES

12:40 PM	x	TH
1:00 PM	x	TH
1:20 PM	x	TH
1:40 PM	x	
2:00 PM		
2:20 PM	x	TH
2:40 PM	x	TH
3:00 PM		
3:20 PM	X	nEV
3:40 PM	X	nEV
4:00 PM	X	nEV

ALISON PETERSON V. GROCERY DEPOT, INC.

DELI DEPEARTMENT FLOOR CHECK REPORT

To all deli department employees:

Three times per hour the deli and produce department floor areas must be inspected for spills, dirt, or any other hazards that may need attention. Someone from the produce department must sign the form below indicating the floor has been inspected. Further, always remain aware of problems that may arise on an on going basis.

March 23, 2011

TIME	PLACE "X" IF INSPECTED	INITIALS
6:00 AM	X	KL
6:20 AM	X	KL
6:40 AM	X	KL
7:00 AM	X	KL
7:20 AM	X	
7:40 AM	X	JO
8:00 AM	X	JO
8:20 AM	X	JO
8:40 AM	X	JO
9:00 AM	X	
9:20 AM	X	NK
9:40 AM	X	NK
10:00 AM	X	NK
10:20 AM		NK
10:40 AM	X	NK
11:00 AM	X	DB
11:20 AM	X	DB
11:40 AM		DB
12:00 PM	X	DB
12:20 PM	X	DB
12:40 PM	X	

SUPPORTING RECORDS, REPORTS AND IMAGES

1:00 PM	X	DB
1:20 PM	X	
1:40 PM	X	DB
2:00 PM	⊥	RR
2:20 PM	⊥	RR
2:40 PM	⊥	RR
3:00 PM	X	DB
3:20 PM	X	DB
3:40 PM	X	DB
4:00 PM	X	MW

GROCERY DEPOT, INC. DELI RECEIPT

GROCERY DEPOT
=== DELI ===

15300 NE Dunes Boulevard
Sunland, Foster 99587

MARCH 23, 2011 1:05PM

1 Medium Soda	.89
1 Small Soda	.59
Total	$1.48

Card Number	XXXX XXXX XXXX 3247
Entry Date	03/23
Merchant ID	034865
Authorization Code	034865
Visa Sale	1.48

Thank You for Choosing
Grocery Depot of Sunland

PLEASE COME AGAIN

SUPPORTING RECORDS, REPORTS AND IMAGES

DRIVERS LICENSES

CLASS: C - Any sincle vehicle with a GVWR of not more than 26,000 pounds with the proper endorsments. Any emergency vehicle operated by a firefighter.

CLASS: C - Any sincle vehicle with a GVWR of not more than 26,000 pounds with the proper endorsments. Any emergency vehicle operated by a firefighter.

ALISON PETERSON V. GROCERY DEPOT, INC.

MIKA DRIVESDALE VISA CARD

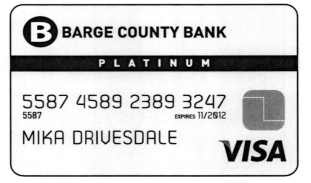

BANANA SIGNAGE
This is a picture of the actual sign used on the day of the incident.

ALISON PETERSON V. GROCERY DEPOT, INC.

SUPPORTING RECORDS, REPORTS AND IMAGES

ALISON PETERSON V. GROCERY DEPOT, INC.

STATE OF FOSTER STATUES AND CASES

STATE OF FOSTER STATUTES AND CASES

STATUES AND CASE FILE

The state of Foster has adopted the statutes referred to as Foster Revised Statutes (FRS) as the current code to be used in all jurisdictions in the state. Also, Foster has agreed that both of the cases in the case file are adopted as current case law and shall be used as precedent case law until the Foster Supreme Court overturns them.

1. Foster Revised Statutes (FRS)
2. Palsgraf v. Long Island Railroad
3. Overpeck v. Roger's Supermarket, LLC
4. Sullivan v. Skate Zone, Inc.
5. Elston v. Circus Circus Mississippi, Inc.

ALISON PETERSON V. GROCERY DEPOT, INC.

FOSTER REVISED STATUTES (FRS)

[FRS 16. A]
"Slip and fall" cases are traditionally based on the duty of care that a possessor of land owes to an invitee. "A business visitor is a person who is invited to enter or remain on land for a purpose directly or indirectly connected with business dealings with the possessor of the land." Restatement (Second) of Torts § 332(3) (A.L.I.1965).

[FRS 16. A.1]
A possessor of land is subject to liability for physical harm caused to his invitees by a condition on the land if, but only if, he:
> [FRS 16. A.1(a)] knows or by the exercise of reasonable care would discover the condition, and should realize that it involves an unreasonable risk of harm to such invitees; and
> [FRS 16. A.1(b)] should expect that they will not discover or realize the danger, or will fail to protect themselves against it; and
> [FRS 16. A.1(c)] fails to exercise reasonable care to protect them against the danger.

[FRS 16. A.2]
Id. at § 343. And, if the possessor of the property holds it open to the public for entry for his business purposes, he is subject to liability to members of the public while they are on the property for business purposes for physical harm caused by the accidental, negligent, or intentionally harmful acts of third persons if the possessor failed to exercise reasonable care to either: a) discover that such acts are being done or are likely to be done, or b) give warning adequate to enable the business visitors to avoid the harm, or otherwise protect them against it. Id. § 344.

[FRS 16. B]
Under these common law principles, the business owner has an affirmative duty to exercise reasonable care to inspect for hazardous conditions.

[FRS 16. C]
The occupier must not only use care not to injure the visitor by negligent activities, and warn him of hidden dangers known to the occupier, but he must also act reasonably to inspect the premises to discover possible dangerous conditions of which he does not know, and take reasonable precautions to protect the invitee from dangers which are foreseeable from the arrangement

or use of the property. William Prosser and W. Page Keeton, Prosser and Keeton on Torts, § 61, at 425-26 (5th ed.1984).

[FRS 16. D]
A PROPRIETOR IS GUILTY OF NEGLIGENCE ONLY IF HE:
 Fails to use reasonable care under the circumstances to discover the foreseeable dangerous condition.
 Fails to correct the condition or to warn customers of its existence.

NOTES
PRINCIPLES OF NOTICE VERSUS DUTY:
Causation and notice should be treated not as elements of the customer's case, but as affirmative defenses of the proprietor. The customer would retain the burden of proving that there was a foreign substance/object on the floor and that such was a substantial factor in causing his accident and injury.

Such proof that the premises were unsafe would avoid a summary judgment or directed verdict and shift to the proprietor the burden of proving that his employees did not cause the substance/object to be on the floor and that it had been there for an insufficient length of time to have been discovered and removed or warned of by his employees.

ALISON PETERSON V. GROCERY DEPOT, INC.

STATE OF FOSTER JURY WORKSHEET

Case # _____

Date _____

NEGLIGENCE WORKSHEET
Please mark each element that has been established

_____ Duty. Was there a duty owed to the plaintiff by the defendant

_____ Breach of the Duty. Was the above duty not performed?

Causation. This is a two part test:

    _____ Actual Cause. Did the defendant actually cause the harm and but for the actions or inactions the plaintiff would not be injured.

    _____ Proximate Cause. Was it foreseeable that the plaintiff would be injured?

_____ Damages. The plaintiff must have real and ascertainable damages.

DEFENSES
The state of Foster only allows for one defense unless the Judge states an additional defense may be used. The defense marked as state of Foster is the adopted and allowed defense, however, two others are listed but shall not be used unless instructed by the Judge.

STATE OF FOSTER STATUTES AND CASES

_____ Comparative Fault. State of Foster. If the plaintiff is found to be at fault, the damages are reduced by the percentage stated:

_____ % Plaintiff fault

_____ % Defendant fault

_____ Assumption of the Risk. If plaintiff assumed the risk, no recovery of damages is allowed

_____ Contributory Negligence. If plaintiff contributed to his/her harm, no recovery of damages is allowed

CHAIRPERSON OF THE JURY STATEMENT

We the jury have found the defendant, _____, blameworthy / not-blameworthy of Negligence and shall / shall-not pay the plaintiff damages.

Final damages awarded $ _____

ALISON PETERSON V. GROCERY DEPOT, INC.

248 N.Y. 339
162 N.E. 99
PALSGRAF
V.
LONG ISLAND R. CO. *
COURT OF APPEALS OF NEW YORK.
MAY 29, 1928.

Action by Helen Palsgraf against the Long Island Railroad Company. Judgment entered on the verdict of a jury in favor of the plaintiff was affirmed by the Appellate Division by a divided court (222 App. Div. 166, 225 N. Y. S. 412), and defendant appeals.

Reversed, and complaint dismissed.

Andrews, Crane, and O'Brien, JJ., dissenting.

[248 N.Y. 339]Appeal from Supreme Court, Appellate Division, Second department. [248 N.Y. 340]William McNamara and Joseph F. Keany, both of New York City, for appellant.

Mathew W. Wood, of New York City, for respondent.

CARDOZO, C. J.

Plaintiff was standing on a platform of defendant's railroad after buying a ticket to go to Rockaway Beach. A train stopped at the station, bound for another place. Two men ran forward to catch it. One of the men reached the platform of the car without mishap, though the train was already moving. The other man, carrying a package, jumped aboard the car, but seemed unsteady as if about to fall. A guard on the car, who had held the door open, reached forward to help [248 N.Y. 341]him in, and another guard on the platform pushed him from behind. In this act, the package was dislodged, and fell upon the rails. It was a package of small size, about fifteen inches long, and was covered by a newspaper. In fact it contained fireworks, but there was nothing in its appearance to give notice of its contents. The fireworks when they fell exploded. The shock of the explosion threw down some scales at the other end of the platform many feet away. The scales struck the plaintiff, causing injuries for which she sues.

[1][2][3] The conduct of the defendant's guard, if a wrong in its relation to the holder of the package, was not a wrong in its relation to the plaintiff, standing far away. Relatively to her it was not negligence at all. Nothing in the situation

gave notice that the falling package had in it the potency of peril to persons thus removed. Negligence is not actionable unless it involves the invasion of a legally protected interest, the violation of a right. 'Proof of negligence in the air, so to speak, will not do.' Pollock, Torts (11th Ed.) p. 455; Martin v. Herzog, 228 N. Y. 164, 170, 126 N. E. 814. Cf. Salmond, Torts (6th Ed.) p. 24. 'Negligence is the absence of care, according to the circumstances.' Willes, J., in Vaughan v. Taff Vale Ry. Co., 5 H. & N. 679, 688; 1 Beven, Negligence (4th Ed.) 7; Paul v. Consol. Fireworks Co., 212 N. Y. 117, 105 N. E. 795;Adams v. Bullock, 227 N. Y. 208, 211, 125 N. E. 93;Parrott v. Wells-Fargo Co., 15 Wall. [U. S.] 524, 21 L. Ed. 206. The plaintiff, as she stood upon the platform of the station, might claim to be protected against intentional invasion of her bodily security. Such invasion is not charged. She might claim to be protected against unintentional invasion by conduct involving in the thought of reasonable men an unreasonable hazard that such invasion would ensue. These, from the point of view of the law, were the bounds of her immunity, with perhaps some rare exceptions, survivals for the most part of ancient forms of liability, where conduct is held to be at the peril of the actor. [248 N.Y. 342]Sullivan v. Dunham, 161 N. Y. 290, 55 N. E. 923,47 L. R. A. 715, 76 Am. St. Rep. 274. If no hazard was apparent to the eye of ordinary vigilance, an act innocent and harmless, at least to outward seeming, with reference to her, did not take to itself the quality of a tort because it happened to be a wrong, though apparently not one involving the risk of bodily insecurity, with reference to some one else. 'In every instance, before negligence can be predicated of a given act, back of the act must be sought and found a duty to the individual complaining,

[162 N.E. 100]

the observance of which would have averted or avoided the injury.' McSherry, C. J., in West Virginia Central & P. R. Co. v. State, 96 Md. 652, 666, 54 A. 669, 671 (61 L. R. A. 574). Cf. Norfolk & W. Ry. Co. v. Wood, 99 Va. 156, 158, 159, 37 S. E. 846;Hughes v. Boston R. R. Co., 71 N. H. 279, 284, 51 A. 1070,93 Am. St. Rep. 518;U. S. Express Co. v. Everest, 72 Kan. 517;1Emry v. Roanoke Navigation & Water Power Co., 111 N. C. 94, 95, 16 S. E. 18,17 L. R. A. 699;Vaughan v. Transit Development Co., 222 N. Y. 79, 118 N. E. 219;Losee v. Clute, 51 N. Y. 494;Di Caprio v. New York Cent. R. Co., 231 N. Y. 94, 131 N. E. 746, 16 A. L. R. 940; 1 Shearman & Redifield on Negligence, § 8, and cases cited; Cooley on Torts (3d Ed.) p. 1411; Jaggard on Torts, vol. 2, p. 826; Wharton, Negligence, § 24; Bohlen, Studies in the Law of Torts, p. 601. 'The ideas of negligence and duty are strictly correlative.' Bowen, L. J., in Thomas v. Quartermaine, 18 Q. B. D.

685, 694. The plaintiff sues in her own right for a wrong personal to her, and not as the vicarious beneficiary of a breach of duty to another.

A different conclusion will involve us, and swiftly too, in a maze of contradictions. A guard stumbles over a package which has been left upon a platform. It seems to be a bundle of newspapers. It turns out to be a can of dynamite. To the eye of ordinary vigilance, the bundle is abandoned waste, which may be kicked or trod on with impunity. Is a passenger at the other end of the platform protected by the law against the unsuspected hazard concealed beneath the waste? If not, is the result to be any different, so far as the distant passenger is concerned, when the guard stumbles over a valise [248 N.Y. 343] which a truckman or a porter has left upon the walk? The passenger far away, if the victim of a wrong at all, has a cause of action, not derivative, but original and primary. His claim to be protected against invasion of his bodily security is neither greater nor less because the act resulting in the invasion is a wrong to another far removed. In this case, the rights that are said to have been violated, are not even of the same order. The man was not injured in his person nor even put in danger. The purpose of the act, as well as its effect, was to make his person safe. It there was a wrong to him at all, which may very well be doubted it was a wrong to a property interest only, the safety of his package. Out of this wrong to property, which threatened injury to nothing else, there has passed, we are told, to the plaintiff by derivation or succession a right of action for the invasion of an interest of another order, the right to bodily security. The diversity of interests emphasizes the futility of the effort to build the plaintiff's right upon the basis of a wrong to some one else. The gain is one of emphasis, for a like result would follow if the interests were the same. Even then, the orbit of the danger as disclosed to the eye of reasonable vigilance would be the orbit of the duty. One who jostles one's neighbor in a crowd does not invade the rights of others standing at the outer fringe when the unintended contact casts a bomb upon the ground. The wrongdoer as to them is the man who carries the bomb, not the one who explodes it without suspicion of the danger. Life will have to be made over, and human nature transformed, before prevision so extravagant can be accepted as the norm of conduct, the customary standard to which behavior must conform.

The argument for the plaintiff is built upon the shifting meanings of such words as 'wrong' and 'wrongful,' and shares their instability. What the plaintiff must [248 N.Y. 344]show is 'a wrong' to herself; i. e., a violation of her own right, and not merely a wrong to some one else, nor conduct 'wrongful' because unsocial, but not 'a wrong' to any one. We are told that one who drives at reckless speed through a crowded city street is guilty of a negligent act and therefore of a wrongful one, irrespective of the consequences. Negligent the act is, and wrongful in the sense that it is unsocial, but wrongful and unsocial in relation to other travelers, only because the eye of vigilance perceives the risk of damage. If the same act were to be committed on a speedway or a race course, it would lose its wrongful quality. The risk reasonably to be perceived defines the duty to be obeyed, and risk imports relation; it is risk to another or to others within the range of apprehension. Seavey, Negligence, Subjective or Objective, 41 H. L. Rv. 6; Boronkay v. Robinson & Carpenter, 247 N. Y. 365, 160 N. E. 400. This does not mean, of course, that one who launches a destructive force is always relieved of liability, if the force, though known to be destructive, pursues an unexpected path. 'It was not necessary that the defendant should have had notice of the particular method in which an accident would occur, if the possibility of an accident was clear to the ordinarily prudent eye.' Munsey v. Webb, 231 U. S. 150, 156, 34 S. Ct. 44, 45 (58 L. Ed. 162);Condran v. Park & Tilford, 213 N. Y. 341, 345,107 N. E. 565;Robert v. United States Shipping Board Emergency Fleet Corp., 240 N. Y. 474, 477, 148 N. E. 650. Some acts, such as shooting are so imminently dangerous to any one who may come within reach of the missile however unexpectedly, as to impose a duty of prevision not far from that of an insurer. Even to-day, and much oftener in earlier stages of the law, one acts

[162 N.E. 101]

sometimes at one's peril. Jeremiah Smith, Tort and Absolute Liability, 30 H. L. Rv. 328; Street, Foundations of Legal Liability, vol. 1, pp. 77, 78. Under this head, it may be, fall certain cases of what is known as transferred intent, an act willfully dangerous to A resulting by misadventure in injury to B. Talmage v. Smith, 101 Mich. 370, 374, 59 N. W. 656,45 Am. St. Rep. 414.[248 N.Y. 345] These cases aside, wrong is defined in terms of the natural or probable, at least when unintentional. Parrot v. Wells-Fargo Co. (The Nitro-Glycerine Case) 15 Wall. 524, 21 L. Ed. 206. The range of reasonable apprehension is at times a question for the court, and at times, if varying inferences are possible, a question for the jury. Here, by concession, there was nothing in the situation to suggest to the most cautious mind that the parcel wrapped in newspaper would spread wreckage through the station. If the guard had thrown it down knowingly and willfully, he would not have threatened the plaintiff's safety, so far as appearances could warn him. His conduct would not have involved, even then, an unreasonable probability of invasion of her bodily security. Liability can be no greater where the act is inadvertent.

[4] Negligence, like risk, is thus a term of relation. Negligence in the abstract, apart from things related, is surely not a tort, if indeed it is understandable at all. Bowen, L. J., in Thomas v. Quartermaine, 18 Q. B. D. 685, 694. Negligence is not a tort unless it results in the commission of a wrong, and the commission of a wrong imports the violation of a right, in this case, we are told, the right to be protected against interference with one's bodily security. But bodily security is protected, not against all forms of interference or aggression, but only against some. One who seeks redress at law does not make out a cause of action by showing without more that there has been damage to his person. If the harm was not willful, he must show that the act as to him had possibilities of danger so many and apparent as to entitle him to be protected against the doing of it though the harm was unintended. Affront to personality is still the keynote of the wrong. Confirmation of this view will be found in the history and development of the action on the case. Negligence as a basis of civil liability was unknown to mediaeval law. 8 Holdsworth, History of English Law, p. 449; Street, Foundations of Legal Liability, vol. 1, [248 N.Y. 346]pp. 189, 190. For damage to the person, the sole remedy was trespass, and trespass did not lie in the absence of aggression, and that direct and personal. Holdsworth, op. cit. p. 453; Street, op. cit. vol. 3, pp. 258, 260, vol. 1, pp. 71, 74. Liability for other damage, as where a servant without orders from the master does or omits something to the damage of another, is a plant of later growth. Holdsworth, op. cit. 450, 457; Wigmore, Responsibility for Tortious Acts, vol. 3, Essays in Anglo-American Legal History, 520, 523, 526, 533. When it emerged out of the legal soil, it was thought of as a variant of trespass, an offshoot of the parent stock. This appears in the form of action, which was known as trespass on the case. Holdsworth, op. cit. p. 449; cf. Scott v. Shepard, 2 Wm. Black. 892; Green, Rationale of Proximate Cause, p. 19. The victim does not sue derivatively, or by right of subrogation, to vindicate an interest invaded in the person of another. Thus to view his cause of action is to ignore the fundamental difference between tort and crime. Holland, Jurisprudence (12th Ed.) p. 328. He sues for breach of a duty owing to himself.

The law of causation, remote or proximate, is thus foreign to the case before us. The question of liability is always anterior to the question of the measure of the consequences that go with liability. If there is no tort to be redressed, there is no occasion to consider what damage might be recovered if there were a finding of a tort. We may assume, without deciding, that negligence, not at large or in the abstract, but in relation to the plaintiff, would entail liability for any and all consequences, however novel or extraordinary. Bird v. St. Paul Fire & Marine Ins. Co., 224 N. Y. 47, 54,120 N. E. 86, 13 A. L. R. 875;Ehrgott v. Mayor, etc., of City of New York, 96 N. Y. 264, 48 Am. Rep. 622;Smith v. London & S. W. R. Co., [1870-1871] L. R. 6 C. P. 14; 1 Beven, Negligence, 106; Street, op. cit. vol. 1, p. 90; Green, Rationale of Proximate Cause, pp. 88, 118; cf. Matter of Polemis, L. R. 1921, 3 K. B. 560; 44 Law Quarterly Review, 142. There is room for [248 N.Y. 347]argument that a distinction is to be drawn according to the diversity of interests invaded by the act, as where conduct negligent in that it threatens an insignificant invasion of an interest in property results in an unforeseeable invasion of an interest of another order, as, e. g., one of bodily security. Perhaps other distinctions may be necessary. We do not go into the question now. The consequences to be followed must first be rooted in a wrong.

The judgment of the Appellate Division and that of the Trial Term should be reversed, and the complaint dismissed, with costs in all courts.

ANDREWS, J. (dissenting).

Assisting a passenger to board a train, the defendant's servant negligently knocked a package from his arms. It fell between the platform and the cars. Of its contents the servant knew and could know nothing. A violent explosion followed. The concussion broke some scales

[162 N.E. 102]

standing a considerable distance away. In falling, they injured the plaintiff, an intending passenger.

Upon these facts, may she recover the damages she has suffered in an action brought against the master? The result we shall reach depends upon our theory as to the nature of negligence. Is it a relative concept-the breach of some duty owing to a particular person or to particular persons? Or, where there is an act which unreasonably threatens the safety of others, is the doer liable for all its proximate consequences, even where they result in injury to one who would generally be thought to be outside the radius of danger? This is not a mere dispute as to words. We might not believe that to the average mind the dropping of the bundle would seem to involve the probability of harm to the plaintiff standing many feet away whatever might be the case as to the owner or to one so near as to be likely to be struck by its fall. If, however, we adopt the second hypothesis,[248 N.Y. 348]we have to inquire only as to the relation between cause and effect. We deal in terms of proximate cause, not of negligence.

Negligence may be defined roughly as an act or omission which unreasonably does or may affect the rights of others, or which unreasonably fails to protect one's self from the dangers resulting from such acts. Here I confine myself to the first branch of the definition. Nor do I comment on the word 'unreasonable.' For present purposes it sufficiently describes that average of conduct that society requires of its members.

There must be both the act or the omission, and the right. It is the act itself, not the intent of the actor, that is important. Hover v. Barkhoof, 44 N. Y. 113;Mertz v. Connecticut Co., 217 N. Y. 475, 112 N. E. 166. In criminal law both the intent and the result are to be considered. Intent again is material in tort actions, where punitive damages are sought, dependent on actual malice-not one merely reckless conduct. But here neither insanity nor infancy lessens responsibility. Williams v. Hays, 143 N. Y. 442, 38 N. E. 449, 26 L. R. A. 153, 42 Am. St. Rep. 743.

As has been said, except in cases of contributory negligence, there must be rights which are or may be affected. Often though injury has occurred, no rights of him who suffers have been touched. A licensee or trespasser upon my land has no claim to affirmative care on my part that the land be made safe. Meiers v. Fred Koch Brewery, 229 N. Y. 10, 127 N. E. 491, 13 A. L. R. 633. Where a railroad is required to fence its tracks against cattle, no man's rights are injured should he wander upon the road because such fence is absent. Di Caprio v. New York Cent. R. Co., 231 N. Y. 94, 131 N. E. 746, 16 A. L. R. 940. An unborn child may not demand immunity from personal harm. Drobner v. Peterson, 232 N. Y. 220, 133 N. E. 567, 20 A. L. R. 1503.

But we are told that 'there is no negligence unless there is in the particular case a legal duty to take care, and this duty must be not which is owed to the plaintiff [248 N.Y. 349]himself and not merely to others.' Salmond Torts (6th Ed.) 24. This I think too narrow a conception. Where there is the unreasonable act, and some right that may be affected there is negligence whether damage

STATE OF FOSTER STATUTES AND CASES

does or does not result. That is immaterial. Should we drive down Broadway at a reckless speed, we are negligent whether we strike an approaching car or miss it by an inch. The act itself is wrongful. If is a wrong not only to those who happen to be within the radius of danger, but to all who might have been there-a wrong to the public at large. Such is the language of the street. Such the language of the courts when speaking of contributory negligence. Such again and again their language in speaking of the duty of some defendant and discussing proximate cause in cases where such a discussion is wholly irrelevant on any other theory. Perry v. Rochester Line Co., 219 N. Y. 60, 113 N. E. 529, L. R. A. 1917B, 1058. As was said by Mr. Justice Holmes many years ago:

"The measure of the defendant's duty in determining whether a wrong has been committed is one thing, the measure of liability when a wrong has been committed is another.' Spade v. Lynn & B. R. Co., 172 Mass. 488, 491, 52 N. E. 747, 748 (43 L. R. A. 832, 70 Am. St. Rep. 298).

Due care is a duty imposed on each one of us to protect society from unnecessary danger, not to protect A, B, or C alone.

It may well be that there is no such thing as negligence in the abstract. 'Proof of negligence in the air, so to speak, will not do.' In an empty world negligence would not exist. It does involve a relationship between man and his fellows, but not merely a relationship between man and those whom he might reasonably expect his act would injure; rather, a relationship between him and those whom he does in fact injure. If his act has a tendency to harm some one, it harms him a mile away as surely as it does those on the scene. We now permit children to recover for the negligent killing of the father. It was never prevented on the theory that no duty was owing to them. A husband may be compensated for [248 N.Y. 350]the loss of his wife's services. To say that the wrongdoer was negligent as to the husband as well as to the wife is merely an attempt to fit facts to theory. An insurance company paying a fire loss recovers

[162 N.E. 103]

its payment of the negligent incendiary. We speak of subrogation-of suing in the right of the insured. Behind the cloud of words is the fact they hide, that the act, wrongful as to the insured, has also injured the company. Even if it be true that the fault of father, wife, or insured will prevent recovery, it is because we consider the original negligence, not the proximate cause of the injury. Pollock, Torts (12th Ed.) 463.

In the well-known Polhemis Case, [1921] 3 K. B. 560, Scrutton, L. J., said that the dropping of a plank was negligent, for it might injure 'workman or cargo or ship.' Because of either possibility, the owner of the vessel was to be made good for his loss. The act being wrongful, the doer was liable for its proximate results. Criticized and explained as this statement may have been, I think it states the law as it should be and as it is. Smith v. London & S. W. R. Co. R. R. (1870-71) L. R. 6 C. P. 14;Anthony v. Staid, 52 Mass. (11 Metc.) 290;Wood v. Pennsylvania R. Co., 177 Pa. 306, 35 A. 699, 35 L. R. A. 199, 55 Am. St. Rep. 728; Trashansky v. Hershkovitz, 239 N. Y. 452, 147 N. E. 63.

The proposition is this: Every one owes to the world at large the duty of refraining from those acts that may unreasonably threaten the safety of others. Such an act occurs. Not only is he wronged to whom harm, might reasonably be expected to result, but he also who is in fact injured, even if he be outside what would generally be thought the danger zone. There needs be duty due the one complaining, but this is not a duty to a particular individual because as to him harm might be expected. Harm to some one being the natural result of the act, not only that one alone, but all those in fact injured may complain. We have never, I think, held otherwise. Indeed in the Di Caprio Case we said that a breach of a [248 N.Y. 351]general ordinance defining the degree of care to be exercised in one's calling is evidence of negligence as to every one. We did not limit this statement to those who might be expected to be exposed to danger. Unreasonable risk being taken, its consequences are not confined to those who might probably be hurt.

If this be so, we do not have a plaintiff suing by 'derivation or succession.' Her action is original and primary. Her claim is for a breach of duty to herself- not that she is subrogated to any right of action of the owner of the parcel or of a passenger standing at the scene of the explosion.

The right to recover damages rests on additional considerations. The plaintiff's rights must be injured, and this injury must be caused by the negligence. We build a dam, but are negligent as to its foundations. Breaking, it injures property down stream. We are not liable if all this happened because of some reason other than the insecure foundation. But, when injuries do result from out unlawful act, we are liable for the consequences. It does not matter that they are unusual, unexpected, unforeseen, and unforeseeable. But there is one limitation. The damages must be so connected with the negligence that the latter may be said to be the proximate cause of the former.

These two words have never been given an inclusive definition. What is a cause in a legal sense, still more what is a proximate cause, depend in each case upon many considerations, as does the existence of negligence itself. Any philosophical doctrine of causation does not help us. A boy throws a stone into a pond. The ripples spread. The water level rises. The history of that pond is altered to all eternity. It will be altered by other causes also. Yet it will be forever the resultant of all causes combined. Each one will have an influence. How great only omniscience can say. You may speak of a chain, or, if you please, a net. An analogy is of little aid. [248 N.Y. 352]Each cause brings about future events. Without each the future would not be the same. Each is proximate in the sense it is essential. But that is not what we mean by the word. Nor on the other hand do we mean sole cause. There is no such thing.

Should analogy be though helpful, however, I prefer that of a stream. The spring, starting on its journey, is joined by tributary after tributary. The river, reaching the ocean, comes from a hundred sources. No man may say whence any drop of water is derived. Yet for a time distinction may be possible. Into the clear creek, brown swamp water flows from the left. Later, from the right comes water stained by its clay bed. The three may remain for a space, sharply divided. But at last inevitably no trace of separation remains. They are so commingled that all distinction is lost.

As we have said, we cannot trace the effect of an act to the end, if end there is. Again, however, we may trace it part of the way. A murder at Serajevo may be the necessary antecedent to an assassination in London twenty years hence. An overturned lantern may burn all Chicago. We may follow the fire from the shed to the last building. We rightly say the fire started by the lantern caused its destruction.

A cause, but not the proximate cause. What we do mean by the word 'proximate' is that, because of convenience, of public policy, of a rough sense of justice, the law arbitrarily declines to trace a series of events beyond a certain point. This is not logic. It is practical politics. Take our rule as to fires. Sparks from my burning haystack set on fire my house and my neighbor's. I may recover from a negligent railroad He may not. Yet the wrongful act as directly harmed the one as the other. We may regret that the line was drawn just where it was, but drawn somewhere it had to be. We said the act of the railroad was not the proximate cause of our neighbor's fire. Cause it surely was. The words we used were [248 N.Y. 353] simply indicative of our notions of public policy. Other courts think differently. But somewhere they reach the point where they cannot say the stream comes from any one source.

Take the illustration given in an unpublished manuscript by a distinguished and helpful writer on the law of torts. A chauffeur negligently collides with another car which is filled with dynamite, although he could not know it. An explosion follows. A, walking on the sidewalk nearby, is killed. B, sitting in a window of a building opposite, is cut by flying glass. C, likewise sitting in a window a block away, is similarly injured. And a further illustration: A nursemaid, ten blocks away, startled by the noise, involuntarily drops a baby from her arms to the walk. We are told that C may not recover while A may. As to B it is a question for court or jury. We will all agree that the baby might not. Because, we are again told, the chauffeur had no reason to believe his conduct involved any risk of injuring either C or the baby. As to them he was not negligent.

But the chauffeur, being negligent in risking the collision, his belief that the scope of the harm he might do would be limited is immaterial. His act unreasonably jeopardized the safety of any one who might be affected by it. C's injury and that of the baby were directly traceable to the collision. Without that, the injury would not have happened. C had the right to sit in his office, secure from such dangers. The baby was entitled to use the sidewalk with reasonable safety.

The true theory is, it seems to me, that the injury to C, if in truth he is to be denied recovery, and the injury to the baby, is that their several injuries were not the proximate result of the negligence. And here not what the chauffeur had reason to believe would be the result of his conduct, but what the prudent would foresee, may have a bearing-may have some bearing, for the problem[248 N.Y. 354]of proximate cause is not to be solved by any one consideration. It is all a question of expediency. There are no fixed rules to govern our judgment. There are simply matters of which we may take account.

STATE OF FOSTER STATUTES AND CASES

We have in a somewhat different connection spoken of 'the stream of events.' We have asked whether that stream was deflected-whether it was forced into new and unexpected channels. Donnelly v. H. C. & A. I. Piercy Contracting Co., 222 N. Y. 210, 118 N. E. 605. This is rather rhetoric than law. There is in truth little to guide us other than common sense.

There are some hints that may help us. The proximate cause, involved as it may be with many other causes, must be, at the least, something without which the event would not happen. The court must ask itself whether there was a natural and continuous sequence between cause and effect. Was the one a substantial factor in producing the other? Was there a direct connection between them, without too many intervening causes? Is the effect of cause on result not too attentuated? Is the cause likely, in the usual judgment of mankind, to produce the result? Or, by the exercise of prudent foresight, could the result be foreseen? Is the result too remote from the cause, and here we consider remoteness in time and space. Bird v. St. Paul & M. Ins. Co., 224 N. Y. 47, 120 N. E. 86, 13 A. L. R. 875, where we passed upon the construction of a contract-but something was also said on this subject. Clearly we must so consider, for the greater the distance either in time or space, the more surely do other causes intervene to affect the result. When a lantern is overturned, the firing of a shed is a fairly direct consequence. Many things contribute to the spread of the conflagration-the force of the wind, the direction and width of streets, the character of intervening structures, other factors. We draw an uncertain and wavering line, but draw it we must as best we can.

Once again, it is all a question of fair judgment, always [248 N.Y. 355] keeping in mind the fact that we endeavor to make a rule in each case that will be practical and in keeping with the general understanding of mankind.

Here another question must be answered. In the case supposed, it is said, and said correctly, that the chauffeur is liable for the direct effect of the explosion, although he had no reason to suppose it would follow a collision. 'The fact that the injury occurred in a different manner than that which might have been expected does not prevent the chauffeur's negligence from being in law the cause of the injury.' But the natural results of a negligent act-the results which a prudent man would or should foresee-do have a bearing upon the decision as to proximate cause. We have said so repeatedly. What should be foreseen? No human foresight would suggest that a collision itself might injure one a block away. On the contrary, given an explosion, such a possibility might be reasonably expected. I think the direct connection, the foresight of which the courts

[162 N.E. 105]

speak, assumes prevision of the explosion, for the immediate results of which, at least, the chauffeur is responsible.

If may be said this is unjust. Why? In fairness he should make good every injury flowing from his negligence. Not because of tenderness toward him we say he need not answer for all that follows his wrong. We look back to the catastrophe, the fire kindled by the spark, or the explosion. We trace the consequences, not indefinitely, but to a certain point. And to aid us in fixing that point we ask what might ordinarily be expected to follow the fire or the explosion.

This last suggestion is the factor which must determine the case before us. The act upon which defendant's liability rests is knocking an apparently harmless package onto the platform. The act was negligent. For its proximate consequences the defendant is liable. If its contents were broken, to the owner; if it fell upon and crushed a passenger's foot, then to him; if it exploded [248 N.Y. 356]and injured one in the immediate vicinity, to him also as to A in the illustration. Mrs. Palsgraf was standing some distance away. How far cannot be told from the record-apparently 25 or 30 feet, perhaps less. Except for the explosion, she would not have been injured. We are told by the appellant in his brief, 'It cannot be denied that the explosion was the direct cause of the plaintiff's injuries.' So it was a substantial factor in producing the result-there was here a natural and continuous sequence-direct connection. The only intervening cause was that, instead of blowing her to the ground, the concussion smashed the weighing machine which in turn fell upon her. There was no remoteness in time, little in space. And surely, given such an explosion as here, it needed no great foresight to predict that the natural result would be to injure one on the platform at no greater distance from its scene than was the plaintiff. Just how no one might be able to predict. Whether by flying fragments, by broken glass, by wreckage of machines or structures no one could say. But injury in some form was most probable.

Under these circumstances I cannot say as a matter of law that the plaintiff's injuries were not the proximate result of the negligence. That is all we have before us. The court refused to so charge. No request was made to submit the matter to the jury as a question of fact, even would that have been proper upon the record before us.

The judgment appealed from should be affirmed, with costs.

POUND, LEHMAN, and KELLOGG, JJ., concur with CARDOZO, C. J.
ANDREWS, J., dissents in opinion in which CRANE and O'BRIEN, JJ., concur.

Judgment reversed, etc.

Notes:
 * Reargument denied 164 N. E. 564.
 183 P. 817.

ALISON PETERSON V. GROCERY DEPOT, INC.

BRIEF OF PALSGRAF V. LONG ISLAND RAILROAD
FACTS OF THE CASE
These are the most basic facts that make up this case that must be known to determine an outcome.

ISSUE
What is the main concern in this case that the court is faced with resolving?

RULE OF LAW
What statues and case law are used to help determine the outcome of this case.

ANALYSIS
This combines the facts with the issue as applied to the rules of law. Be careful to pull this apart one element at a time.

CONCLUSION
This is a simple statement of which party won

STATE OF FOSTER STATUTES AND CASES

Summary of the points in this case that you can use to either support your case or plan a defense.

FIRST STEP
Number every paragraph in the case. Even if the paragraph is only one sentence, number it so you may make a reference to it if needed.

SECOND STEP
In the margin write "Test" if the court is applying a test. If there are multiple parts to the test, mark the elements as follows, "T-1, T-2, T-3, ..." If there is more than one Test in the case, mark the second Test and elements as follows, "Test-2, T2-1, T2-2, T2-3, ..."

THIRD STEP
In the margin mark the final Holding of the case with "Held" and underline the key phrases.

FOURTH STEP
List the parts of this case that you will need to work with to support or plan a defense for your case. Use the paragraph numbers and test numbers you have just finished putting on the case itself for referencing back to the case.

List your case parts, phrases and references below:

1.

2.

ALISON PETERSON V. GROCERY DEPOT, INC.

3.

4.

5.

6.

7.

STATE OF FOSTER STATUTES AND CASES

JOLYNNE OVERPECK and SHANE OVERPECK PLAINTIFFS
v.
ROGER'S SUPERMARKET, LLC DEFENDANT
CAUSE NO.: 1:12-CV-124-SA-DAS
UNITED STATES DISTRICT COURT FOR THE NORTHERN DISTRICT OF
MISSISSIPPI ABERDEEN DIVISION
SO ORDERED: August 21, 2013

MEMORANDUM OPINION

Presently before the Court is Defendant's Motion for Summary Judgment [40]. For the reasons set forth below, that motion is granted in part and denied in part.

Factual and Procedural Background

The present controversy arises out of a slip and fall incident occurring at Roger's Supermarket on September 27, 2011. Plaintiffs Jolynne Overpeck and Shane Overpeck, husband and wife, travelled to Roger's Supermarket on the subject date in order to purchase a beef brisket for a barbecue. As Jolynne Overpeck was surveying the meat selection, she allegedly slipped on a liquid substance near the base of the meat cooler. Although Overpeck was unable to identify the substance, she alleges that it was roughly the size of a dinner plate in diameter and was slightly discolored. She recounts that it had no discernible odor and does not recall the liquid getting on her clothing. Prior to the fall, Overpeck had previously passed through the same section, but had not noticed any liquid on the floor. Shane Overpeck, who had been browsing in another portion of the store, quickly came to his wife's aid. However, he too was unable to positively identify the substance.

After the fall, supermarket employees responded to the area and attempted to both aid Overpeck and to clean up the potential hazard. Kevin Suggs, the assistant manager in the meat department, testified that he called a store manager over to the department and began cleaning up the spill once he was made aware of the situation.

Although no supermarket employee testified that the substance could be positively identified, a number of employees believed that the liquid might have been chicken juice. Further, shortly after the incident, store co-owner Brian Garner sent himself an email stating that Overpeck "slipped and fell on some chicken juice on floor."

According to store employees, chicken is restocked at the supermarket on a daily basis. The chicken is often shipped to the store in bulk and then repackaged into individual Styrofoam containers for retail sale. Roger's employee Sandra Rogers, who is in charge of running the wrapping machine and often stocks the meat cooler, testified that she recalls re-stocking the chicken supply approximately thirty to forty minutes before Overpeck's fall. Rogers also testified that she used one of the meat department's shopping carts to transport the chicken and that, although she could not positively attest, she likely placed butcher paper in the bottom of the cart before wheeling it into the retail area of the store. Further, Rogers denied that the liquid could be attributed to her actions in stocking the chicken, stating that "when you first bring it out, you know it's packaged good and it's not juicy because they prevent—they use everything, you know, to drain the chicken before they tray it up."

Nonetheless, other store employees testified that chicken is prone to leak, and that juices occasionally need to be wiped up in the meat department of the retail area. Additionally, employees also stated that the store adopted a policy of lining the meat department stocking carts with butcher paper to avoid employee-created drips during stocking, and Rogers could not affirmatively recall whether she had lined the buggy on the day in question.

Defendant has filed the present motion for summary judgment arguing that Plaintiffs cannot, as a matter of law, establish that Defendant either breached its duty of care or caused an

unreasonably dangerous condition. Plaintiffs, on the other hand, argue that there is sufficient evidence for a jury to conclude that Defendant either caused the dangerous condition or had actual knowledge of the danger and failed to warn of its presence.

Summary Judgment Standard

Summary judgment is warranted under Rule 56(a) of the Federal Rules of Civil Procedure when the evidence reveals no genuine dispute regarding any material fact, and the moving party is entitled to judgment as a matter of law. The rule "mandates the entry of summary judgment, after adequate time for discovery and upon motion, against a party who fails to make a showing sufficient to establish the existence of an element essential to that party's case, and on which that party will bear the burden of proof at trial." Celotex Corp. v. Catrett, 477 U.S. 317, 322, 106 S. Ct. 2548, 91 L. Ed. 2d 265 (1986).

The party moving for summary judgment "bears the initial responsibility of informing the district court of the basis for its motion, and identifying those portions of [the record] which it believes demonstrate the absence of a genuine issue of material fact." Id. at 323, 106 S. Ct 2548. The nonmoving party must then "go beyond the pleadings" and "designate 'specific facts showing that there is a genuine issue for trial.'" Id. at 324, 106 S. Ct. 2548 (citation omitted). In reviewing the evidence, factual controversies are to be resolved in favor of the nonmovant, "but only when . . . both parties have submitted evidence of contradictory facts." Little v. Liquid Air Corp., 37 F.3d 1069, 1075 (5th Cir. 1994) (en banc). When such contradictory facts exist, the Court may "not make credibility determinations or weigh the evidence." Reeves v. Sanderson Plumbing Prods., Inc., 530 U.S. 133, 150, 120 S. Ct. 2097, 147 L. Ed. 2d 105 (2000). However, conclusory allegations, speculation, unsubstantiated assertions, and legalistic arguments have never constituted an adequate substitute for specific facts showing a genuine

Page 4

issue for trial. TIG Ins. Co. v. Sedgwick James of Wash., 276 F.3d 754, 759 (5th Cir. 2002); SEC v. Recile, 10 F.3d 1093, 1097 (5th Cir. 1997); Little, 37 F.3d at 1075.

Discussion and Analysis

"Premises liability analysis under Mississippi law requires three determinations: (1) legal status of the injured person, (2) relevant duty of care, and (3) defendant's compliance with that duty." Wood v. RIH Acquisitions MS II LLC, 556 F.3d 274, 275 (5th Cir. 2009) (citing Massey v. Tingle, 867 So. 2d

235, 239 (Miss. 2004)). In the present case, it is undisputed that Plaintiff was a business invitee at the time of her accident. Accordingly, the owner or lessee had a duty to keep the business premises "reasonably safe and to warn of any dangerous condition that [was] not readily apparent." Parker v. Wal-Mart Stores, Inc., 261 F. App'x 724, 725-26 (5th Cir. 2008). However, the owner or lessee "is not an insurer of the safety of its invitees," and it is "only liable for injuries caused by a condition that is unreasonably dangerous." Id. at 726.

In order to ultimately recover in an action such as this, Plaintiff must espouse one of three theories: (1) that defendant's own negligence created a dangerous condition which caused plaintiff's injury; (2) that defendant had actual knowledge of a dangerous condition but failed to adequately warn plaintiff of the danger she faced; or (3) that, based upon the passage of time, defendant had constructive knowledge of the condition but failed to adequately warn plaintiff of the danger she faced. K-Mart Corp. v. Hardy ex rel. Hardy, 735 So. 2d 975, 980 (Miss. 1999). The Court addresses those potential avenues individually.

A. Defendant's Own Negligence

When the alleged dangerous condition is caused by the operator's own negligence, a plaintiff need not show the defendant's knowledge of the situation. Jerry Lee's Grocery, Inc., v. Thompson, 528 So. 2d 293, 295 (Miss. 1998). But, to show that the defendant's own negligence

Page 5

created the unreasonably dangerous condition, the facts must provide support for more than mere speculation. See, eg, Munford, Inc., v. Fleming, 597 So. 2d 1282, 1285 (Miss. 1992); Elston v. Circus Circus Mississippi, Inc., 908 So. 2d 771, 774 (Miss. Ct. App. 2005). After all, in order to recover, the plaintiff bears the "burden of presenting significant, probative evidence that [defendant] was not only negligent, but also that such negligence was the proximate cause of the dangerous condition that resulted in [the alleged injury]." K-Mart v. Hardy ex rel. Hardy, 735 So. 2d at 981. Determining whether sufficient proof exists to draw such a conclusion requires the court to carefully examine the factual circumstances leading up to the alleged accident.

Illustratively, in Munford, the Mississippi Supreme Court analyzed a claim that was somewhat analogous to that presented here. 597 So. 2d at 1283. There, the plaintiff slipped in a puddle of water that had leaked from a bottle of spring water on a nearby display shelf. Id. Although the store attendant testified that the employees were indeed responsible for shelving the water, she maintained that she had never placed a leaking bottle on a shelf and had not shelved any bottles in a way that would have caused a leak. Id. at 1285. Additionally, the store attendant testified that during the two to three hours between the time she had last checked the aisle and the fall, at least twenty-five to thirty customers had been through the store. Id. Nonetheless, the Mississippi Supreme Court found that sufficient factual support existed for the jury to reasonably conclude that the employee's own negligence, rather than the actions of a customer, created the danger. Id.

Similarly, in K-Mart v. Hardy, the Court addressed another sufficiency of the evidence dispute in an analogous context. 735 So. 2d at 981. In Hardy, the plaintiff slipped in a puddle of paint located near a display of tiered paint cans at the end-cap of an aisle. Id. at 978. The plaintiff testified that after falling, he observed an open paint can that had fallen on the floor and

created a two to three foot puddle of paint. Id. In support of his theory that one of the defendant's employees had constructed the display in a faulty manner, the plaintiff relied exclusively on circumstantial evidence. Id. at 981.

In support of his case, the plaintiff produced evidence indicating that the paint cans were placed on the display by defendant's employees, that, according to the merchandizing manager, displaying the cans in such a manner without necessary shelving material would have been unsafe, that the paint plaintiff slipped on was identical to that stacked on the display, and that the puddle was close in proximity to the subject display. Id. at 982. In reviewing the judgment, the court held that "[w]hile upon this evidence the jury could have found that someone other than [defendant's] employee was responsible for the paint spill, it was also possible that the jury...found [defendant's] employee improperly stacked the end-cap display or failed to place shelving material between the necessary levels of paint cans causing the paint can to fall from the display." Id. Thus, the court found that the plaintiff had not only met his burden of proof, but had provided "ample evidence" for the jury to find on his behalf. Id.

In the case at hand, the Court finds that there remains a genuine dispute of material fact as to Plaintiff's negligence theory. First, Plaintiff has produced significant evidence supporting her theory that the liquid she slipped upon was chicken juice. Several employees recalled that the general consensus following the accident was that it might have been chicken juice and one of the store owners memorialized that finding in an email he sent to himself. Moreover, supermarket employee Sandra Rogers testified that she restocked chicken approximately thirty to forty minutes prior to the fall and used a shopping cart to wheel the chicken to the retail area. Although she indicated that she believes she would have ensured the bottom of the cart was covered with paper to prevent dripping, she could not recall whether she had actually done so.

Page 7

Further, though she testified that "when you first bring it out, you know, it's packaged good and it's not juicy," she also indicated that spills occasionally need to be cleaned up, and another supermarket employee testified that chicken is the type of meat most likely to leak. Finally, another meat department employee testified that customers are unlikely to punch holes in the meat packaging and agreed that if one was leaking, it was likely just a leaky pack of chicken. The Court therefore finds a genuine dispute of material fact exists as to whether a supermarket employee caused an unreasonably dangerous condition.

B. Constructive Knowledge

As previously articulated, a plaintiff may also recover in a slip and fall case by successfully showing that, based upon the passage of time, the defendant had constructive knowledge of the condition but failed to adequately warn the plaintiff of the danger she faced. Hardy, 735 So. 2d at 980. In the case at hand, Defendant's motion for summary judgment likewise attacks Plaintiff's ability to establish liability under a constructive knowledge theory. Although Plaintiff's complaint indeed sets forth a constructive knowledge theory for recovery, Plaintiff's response to the motion for summary judgment focuses only on Defendant's own negligence and Defendant's actual knowledge of the condition. The Court therefore considers Plaintiff's constructive knowledge theory abandoned and grants Defendant's motion for summary judgment as to that contention. Keenan v. Tejada, 290 F.3d 252, 262 (5th Cir. 2002) ("If a party fails to assert a legal reason why summary judgment should not be granted, that ground is waived and cannot be considered or raised on appeal."); Sanders v. Sailormen, Inc., 2012 WL 663021, at *3 (S.D. Miss. Feb. 28, 2012) ("Failure to address a claim results in the abandonment thereof.").

C. Actual Knowledge

Finally, state law also allows recovery where the defendant had actual knowledge of a dangerous condition but failed to adequately warn plaintiff of the danger she faced. Hardy, 735 So. 2d at 980. Plaintiff here, however, has put forth no factual support for such a theory. As previously articulated by the court, "[t]he standard is whether the defendant had actual knowledge." Sullivan v. Skate Zone, Inc., 946 SO. 2d 828, 832 (Miss. Ct. App. 2007) (citing Anderson v. BH Acquisition, Inc., 771 So. 2d 914, 918 (Miss. 2000)). Plaintiff does not point to any evidence establishing that a Roger's employee actually knew that chicken juice had spilled on the floor prior to Overpeck's fall. Further, to the extent that Plaintiff may be attempting to rely on a mode of operation or proof of prior incidents to support a finding as to Roger's actual knowledge, those theories are equally without merit. First, the court has emphatically rejected a mode of operation theory of recovery, finding that it runs afoul of the well-established rule that property owners are not insurers of the safety of invitees. Sullivan, 946 So. 2d at 832 (citing Byrne v. Wal-Mart Stores, Inc., 877 So. 2d 462, 466-67 (Miss. Ct. App. 2003)).

Second, as to potential prior instances involving chicken juice in the meat department, such instances may be admitted to satisfy the plaintiff's burden only when the other accidents "happened under substantially the same circumstances" and "were not too remote in time from the accident at issue." Bonner v. Imperial Palace of Mississippi, — So. 3d —, 2013 WL 3607165, *7 (Miss. Ct. App. 2013) (citing Irby v. Travis, 935 So. 2d 884, 895 (Miss. 2006)). Plaintiff has completely failed to allege sufficient factual information to gauge either the factual circumstances regarding any other alleged instances or the temporal proximity of such incidents. Summary judgment is therefore also granted as to Plaintiff's actual knowledge theory of recovery. Little v. Liquid Air Corp., 37 F.3d 1069, 1076 (5th Cir. 1994) (holding that a dispute of material fact is not created by metaphysical doubt, conclusory allegations, or unsubstantiated assertions).

D. Loss of Cosortium

Defendant also seeks summary judgment as to Shane Overpeck's loss of consortium claim on grounds that it is completely derivative of his wife's claim. Because Jolynne Overpeck's negligence claim survives the motion for summary judgment and Defendant provides no further attack, Shane Overpeck's loss of consortium claim also survives.

Conclusion

For the foregoing reasons, Defendant's Motion for Summary Judgment is granted in part and denied in part [40]. Because there remains a genuine dispute of material fact as to Plaintiff's premises liability claim based on Defendant's own alleged negligence, the Court denies summary judgment as to that theory. However, finding that judgment as a matter of law is due in favor of Defendant as to Plaintiff's actual and constructive knowledge allegations, the Court grants Defendant's motion as those theories.

Sharion Aycock
United States District Judge

ALISON PETERSON V. GROCERY DEPOT, INC.

BRIEF OF JOLYNNE OVERPECK V. ROGER'S SUPERMARKET, LLC
FACTS OF THE CASE
These are the most basic facts that make up this case that must be known to determine an outcome.

ISSUE
What is the main concern in this case that the court is faced with resolving?

RULE OF LAW
What statues and case law are used to help determine the outcome of this case.

ANALYSIS
This combines the facts with the issue as applied to the rules of law. Be careful to pull this apart one element at a time.

CONCLUSION
This is a simple statement of which party won

STATE OF FOSTER STATUTES AND CASES

Summary of the points in this case that you can use to either support your case or plan a defense.

FIRST STEP
Number every paragraph in the case. Even if the paragraph is only one sentence, number it so you may make a reference to it if needed.

SECOND STEP
In the margin write "Test" if the court is applying a test. If there are multiple parts to the test, mark the elements as follows, "T-1, T-2, T-3, ..." If there is more than one Test in the case, mark the second Test and elements as follows, "Test-2, T2-1, T2-2, T2-3, ..."

THIRD STEP
In the margin mark the final Holding of the case with "Held" and underline the key phrases.

FOURTH STEP
List the parts of this case that you will need to work with to support or plan a defense for your case. Use the paragraph numbers and test numbers you have just finished putting on the case itself for referencing back to the case.

List your case parts, phrases and references below:

1.

2.

ALISON PETERSON V. GROCERY DEPOT, INC.

3.

4.

5.

6.

7.

STATE OF FOSTER STATUTES AND CASES

ALISON PETERSON V. GROCERY DEPOT, INC.

946 SO.2D 828
MICHELLE SULLIVAN AND JEFFREY SULLIVAN, APPELLANTS
V.
SKATE ZONE, INC., APPELLEE.
NO. 2005-CA-01797-COA.
COURT OF APPEALS OF MISSISSIPPI.
JANUARY 16, 2007.
[946 SO.2D 829]
JULIE LYNN LOVE, ATTORNEY FOR APPELLANTS.
JASON RICHARD BUSH, WALKER (BILL) JONES, JACKSON, ATTORNEYS FOR APPELLEE.
BEFORE KING, C.J., IRVING AND GRIFFIS, JJ.
KING, C.J., FOR THE COURT.

1. Michelle and Jeffrey Sullivan appeal the Lowndes County Circuit Court's grant of summary judgment in favor of Skate Zone, Inc. in a premises liability action. The Sullivans raise the following issues on appeal, which we quote verbatim:

I. Whether the trial court erred in granting summary judgment because the defendant created the hazardous condition which caused bodily injury to the plaintiff, Michelle Sullivan, and no proof of actual notice of this particular item being on the floor is required.

II. Whether the trial court erred in granting summary judgment because the defendant expressly admits it failed to warn patrons of a known hazardous condition.

III. Whether the trial court erred in granting summary judgment because the plaintiff proffered evidence the defendant should have known this specific toy was on the rink floor.

IV. Whether the trial court erred in granting summary judgment when there is clear and convincing evidence to support an award of punitive damages.

Finding no error, we affirm the trial court's grant of summary judgment.

FACTS

2. On June 5, 2003, Michelle Sullivan and several family members arrived at Skate Zone, a roller skating rink, in Columbus at approximately 7:00 p.m. At approximately 7:35 p.m., Sullivan was backwards skating with her son when she skated over what she believed to be a two-inch plastic toy and fell to the ground.
[946 So.2d 830]

STATE OF FOSTER STATUTES AND CASES

Sullivan instructed her son to dispose of the toy. Sullivan's sister drove Sullivan to the emergency room at Baptist Golden Triangle Hospital where it was determined that Sullivan had broken her right arm.

3. On June 11, 2004, Sullivan filed a premises liability lawsuit against Skate Zone. Her husband, Michael, submitted a claim for loss of consortium. On May 2, 2005, Skate Zone filed a motion for summary judgment. The Sullivans responded on May 20, 2005. The trial court heard oral argument on the motion for summary judgment on August 15, 2005 and granted summary judgment without written opinion one week later.

ANALYSIS

4. This Court employs the de novo standard when reviewing grants of summary judgment. Moss v. Batesville Casket Co., 935 So.2d 393, 398(15) (Miss. 2006). The moving party has the burden of establishing through pleadings, depositions, answers to interrogatories, admissions, and affidavits that no genuine issue as to any material fact exists. Id. at (16). If the movant proves such, he is entitled to summary judgment as a matter of law. Id. However, the evidence must be viewed in the light most favorable to the non-moving party. Id. at (17).

5. In order for an invitee to succeed in a premises liability action, the invitee must either prove that a negligent act of the property owner caused the invitee's injury or that a third party created a dangerous condition of which the property owner knew or should have known. Grammar v. Dollar, 911 So.2d 619, 624(12) (Miss.Ct.App.2005) (citing Anderson v. B.H. Acquisition Inc., 771 So.2d 914, 918 (8) (Miss.2000)). Sullivan asserts all three basis of premises liability.

I. Whether Skate Zone Caused a Dangerous Condition

6. Sullivan does not argue that a Skate Zone employee actually caused the toy to be on the skating rink. Rather, she argues that Skate Zone breached its duty of keeping the premises in a reasonably safe condition by failing to prevent the toys distributed in the adjacent arcade from being thrown onto the rink.1 The thrust of Sullivan's first argument is that Skate Zone was aware that toys from the arcade could be thrown onto the rink, Skate Zone employed floor guards whose primary responsibility was to inspect the rink and to monitor the activity of patrons, and Skate Zone did not have a floor guard on duty the night of Sullivan's fall.

7. Sullivan argues that the case sub judice is identical to the case of Elston v. Circus Circus Miss., Inc., 908 So.2d 771 (Miss.Ct.App.2005). In Elston, the plaintiff slipped in the casino lobby on a puddle of water in the immediate vicinity of some decorative plants near the front desk. Elston argued that the casino was negligent for either creating the dangerous condition or for having constructive knowledge of the dangerous condition and failing to cure

it. The trial court granted summary judgment in favor of the casino. This Court reversed, finding that genuine issues of material fact existed regarding each theory of liability. Regarding the question of whether the casino created the dangerous condition, the Court found that the lobby plants were watered on a regular basis;

[946 So.2d 831]

the casino retained two employees whose sole responsibility it was to canvas the lobby floor twice per hour to ensure that no debris nor spills were present on the lobby floor; and all employees, regardless of job description, were required to clean spills and debris on the lobby floor. The Court found that although the casino had an established procedure for ensuring that the premises were kept in a reasonably safe condition, the casino could not establish that any employee had inspected the lobby floor on the day of Elston's fall, thereby creating a genuine issue of material fact.

8. Sullivan equates Skate Zone's distribution of prizes in the nearby arcade with the casino's watering of the lobby plants. However, whereas in Elston a jury could have found the puddle on which Elston slipped was caused by a casino employee watering the nearby plants, Sullivan does not even argue that a Skate Zone employee actually caused the plastic object to be on the skating rink floor. Furthermore, unlike Elston, the testimony of Skate Zone's manager established that the rink had been inspected less than one hour prior to Sullivan's fall, and that the manager continued to monitor the floor throughout the skating session.

9. Sullivan also argues that Skate Zone was negligent for not having a floor guard on duty on the evening of her fall. Property owners owe invitees a duty to keep the premises in a reasonably safe condition but are not insurers of invitees' safety. Leffler v. Sharp, 891 So.2d 152, 156(12) (Miss.2004). Skate Zone has a maximum capacity of 1,065 patrons. Elbert Kimbrell, Skate Zone's general manager, testified that he puts one floor guard on duty per every 200 skaters. On slower nights he serves as a floor guard. Sullivan's fall occurred on a Monday night when Skate Zone had approximately 77 patrons skating. Kimbrell testified that he monitored the rink from a disc jockey booth that overlooks the rink and did not see any debris on the floor during the time frame in which Sullivan approximated that she fell. Furthermore, Kimbrell testified that he personally inspected the floors at 6:45 p.m., fifteen minutes before Skate Zone reopened for its second session and approximately fifty minutes before Sullivan fell, and testified that the floors were still clean from being

dust-mopped after the close of the earlier session.

10. "The basis of liability is negligence and not injury. Proof merely of the occurrence of a fall on a floor within business premises is insufficient to show negligence on the part of the proprietor." Byrne v. Wal-Mart Stores, Inc., 877 So.2d 462, 465(6) (Miss.Ct.App.2003) (quoting Sears, Roebuck & Co. v. Tisdale, 185 So.2d 916, 917 (Miss. 1966)). Sullivan failed to produce any proof that the object which caused her fall was on the rink because of any act or omission of Skate Zone. Summary judgment was properly granted as to this theory of premises liability.

II. Whether Skate Zone failed to warn patrons of a known hazardous condition

11. As previously stated, Kimbrell expressly testified that he saw no debris on the skating rink prior to Sullivan's fall. Sullivan did not present proof of any other employee's knowledge of the plastic object's presence on the rink. Instead, Sullivan argues that the fact Skate Zone utilizes a floor guard to police the rink and pick up debris evidences the fact that "Skate Zone was clearly on notice the rink floor is particularly susceptible to these objects being thrown on the floor." Additionally, Sullivan claims that Kimbrell had actual knowledge of the hazard, citing

[946 So.2d 832]

to the following exchange from his deposition:

Q. Would it be fair to say that anywhere you got your 42-inch rail, it would be possible for a patron to toss a small object of any kind onto that floor, wouldn't it?

A. Yes, ma'am. It is.

Q. It does happen from time to time, doesn't it?

A. Yes, ma'am.

Q. It is one of the known hazards of running a skating rink?

A. Yes, ma'am. That's part of it.

Sullivan misunderstands the second basis for premises liability. The standard is whether the defendant had actual knowledge of a dangerous condition and failed to warn the plaintiff. Anderson, 771 So.2d at 918(8). Sullivan showed no more than it was possible for various objects to find their way onto the skating rink.

12. Sullivan is essentially presenting the "mode of operation" argument for premises liability which has been previously rejected by this Court. Under the "mode of operation" theory of premises liability, "when an owner of a self-service establishment has actual notice that his mode of operation creates

certain risks of harm to customers, and those risks are foreseeable, it is not necessary for the plaintiff to prove notice of the hazard that caused the injury." Byrne v. Wal-Mart Stores, Inc., 877 So.2d 462, 466-67(11) (Miss.Ct.App. 2003). In Byrne, the Court concluded that "by accepting Byrne's argument, we would be subjecting store owners who allow customers to walk around the store with food, toys or other potentially `dangerous objects' to a strict liability standard." Id. at 467 (12). This theory is simply inconsistent with the well-established principle that property owners owe invitees a duty of reasonable care to keep the premises in a reasonably safe condition, not to ensure that the premises are completely risk-free. Id.

13. The trial court was also correct in granting summary judgment under the actual knowledge theory of premises liability.

III. Whether Skate Zone had constructive knowledge of a dangerous condition.

14. Constructive knowledge exists where a dangerous condition exists for such a length of time that an owner exercising reasonable care should be alerted to its presence. Anderson, 771 So.2d at 918(10) (citing Drennan v. Kroger Co., 672 So.2d 1168, 1170 (Miss.1996)). Sullivan attempted to prove that the plastic object may have been on the rink floor for some time by testifying that the plastic object appeared to be chipped and scuffed. However, Sullivan also testified that she had skated around the rink several times before falling and had not seen the object until after she fell. Sullivan's son also speculated that the object may have chipped when his mother tripped over it. Also, Skate Zone employees had swept the floor prior to the 7:00 p.m. opening, and Elbert had inspected the rink less than one hour before Sullivan's fall to ensure no debris was on the rink floor. Elbert also testified that he monitored the floor from the disc jockey booth and saw no debris on the floor. We find a total lack of evidence existed to determine how the plastic object came to be on the skating rink floor or how long it had been there. The trial court was also correct in granting summary judgment under the constructive knowledge theory of premises liability.

15. Because we find that summary judgment was properly granted, we decline to address the issue concerning punitive damages.

16. THE JUDGMENT OF THE LOWNDES COUNTY CIRCUIT COURT

[946 So.2d 833]

IS AFFIRMED. ALL COSTS OF THIS APPEAL ARE ASSESSED TO THE APPELLANTS.
LEE AND MYERS, P.JJ., IRVING, CHANDLER, GRIFFIS, BARNES, ISHEE AND ROBERTS, JJ., CONCUR. CARLTON, J., NOT PARTICIPATING.

STATE OF FOSTER STATUTES AND CASES

Notes:
1. The arcade contains "redemption games" in which a patron receives a certain number of tickets according to how skillfully he has played the game. The patron can then redeem his accumulated tickets for small prizes. Sullivan opines that the small plastic object she tripped on was a prize from the arcade.

ALISON PETERSON V. GROCERY DEPOT, INC.

BRIEF OF SULLIVAN V. SKATE ZONE, INC.
FACTS OF THE CASE
These are the most basic facts that make up this case that must be known to determine an outcome.

ISSUE
What is the main concern in this case that the court is faced with resolving?

RULE OF LAW
What statues and case law are used to help determine the outcome of this case.

ANALYSIS
This combines the facts with the issue as applied to the rules of law. Be careful to pull this apart one element at a time.

CONCLUSION
This is a simple statement of which party won

STATE OF FOSTER STATUTES AND CASES

Summary of the points in this case that you can use to either support your case or plan a defense.

FIRST STEP
Number every paragraph in the case. Even if the paragraph is only one sentence, number it so you may make a reference to it if needed.

SECOND STEP
In the margin write "Test" if the court is applying a test. If there are multiple parts to the test, mark the elements as follows, "T-1, T-2, T-3, ..." If there is more than one Test in the case, mark the second Test and elements as follows, "Test-2, T2-1, T2-2, T2-3, ..."

THIRD STEP
In the margin mark the final Holding of the case with "Held" and underline the key phrases.

FOURTH STEP
List the parts of this case that you will need to work with to support or plan a defense for your case. Use the paragraph numbers and test numbers you have just finished putting on the case itself for referencing back to the case.

List your case parts, phrases and references below:
1.

2.

3.

4.

5.

6.

7.

STATE OF FOSTER STATUTES AND CASES

908 SO.2D 771
LINDA ELSTON AND DANNY ELSTON, APPELLANTS
V.
CIRCUS CIRCUS MISSISSIPPI, INC. D/B/A GOLD STRIKE CASINO RESORT AND CIRCUS CIRCUS ENTERPRISES, INC. D/B/A GOLD STRIKE CASINO, APPELLEES.
NO. 2003-CA-02584-COA.
COURT OF APPEALS OF MISSISSIPPI.
FEBRUARY 15, 2005.
REHEARING DENIED MAY 3, 2005.
CERTIORARI DENIED AUGUST 18, 2005.

[908 So.2d 772]

Sara Bailey Russo, Daniel M. Czamanske, Clarksdale, attorneys for appellants.

John Ramsey McCarroll, Andrea Dallas McNeil, Southaven, Eugenia G. McGown, attorneys for appellees.

Before KING, C.J., CHANDLER and ISHEE, JJ.

CHANDLER, J., for the Court.

1. Linda Elston was walking in the lobby of the Gold Strike Casino in Tunica when she slipped in a puddle of water, next to some live plants. Mrs. Elston and her husband sued Gold Strike for her injuries, alleging that Gold Strike created an unreasonably dangerous condition by leaving water on the floor, or alternatively, that the water was left on the floor for a sufficient period of time as to give Gold Strike constructive knowledge of the water on the floor. The Tunica County Circuit Court granted Gold Strike's motion for summary judgment because it found that the Elstons did not present sufficient proof connecting the water on the floor to the act of the plants being watered, and because they produced no evidence to establish the length of time the water was on the floor. The Elstons appeal, raising the following issue:

WHETHER THE CIRCUIT COURT ERRED IN GRANTING GOLD STRIKE'S MOTION FOR SUMMARY JUDGMENT

2. We find that summary judgment was prematurely granted. Accordingly, we

reverse and remand.

FACTS

3. Linda Elston was injured when she entered the hotel lobby of Circus Circus Mississippi, Inc., d/b/a Gold Strike Casino Resort, in Tunica. She encountered a puddle of water which caused her to slip and fall. The fall occurred in the immediate vicinity of some plants and within ten feet of the front desk. As a result of the fall, Mrs. Elston fell on her leg and popped her knee.

4. At the time of her fall, a bellman named Richard Magsby was escorting Mrs. Elston to her hotel room and pointing out the various attractions in the casino. Magsby was walking beside Mrs. Elston.

5. According to Magsby, the plants at Gold Strike are usually watered every Thursday, the day this accident occurred. These plants are usually watered some time between 10:00 a.m. and 11:00 a.m. Mrs. Elston's fall occurred between 1:45 p.m. and 2:45 p.m. Magsby is present in the lobby throughout the day and often observes the plants being watered, but he did not see the plants being watered on the day of Mrs. Elston's accident.

6. Mrs. Elston and her husband sued Gold Strike, alleging that the casino was negligent either by causing a dangerous condition, or that Gold Strike had knowledge

[908 So.2d 773]

that the floor was wet and failed to remedy the dangerous condition which led to Mrs. Elston's injuries. The Tunica County Circuit Court granted Gold Strike's motion for summary judgment, finding that the only thing that had been shown is that Mrs. Elston fell on water that was present in the lobby of the casino. The judge found that the Elstons did not present any evidence beyond speculation connecting the water on the floor to the act of the plants being watered. He also found that the Elstons failed to establish that Gold Strike had knowledge of the dangerous condition, because no one saw water on the floor prior to the accident, and it had not been shown how long the water had been on the floor.

ALISON PETERSON V. GROCERY DEPOT, INC.

ANALYSIS

WHETHER THE CIRCUIT COURT ERRED IN GRANTING GOLD STRIKE'S MOTION FOR SUMMARY JUDGMENT

7. Summary judgment is appropriate "if the pleadings, depositions, answers to interrogatories and admissions on file, together with the affidavits, if any, show that there is no genuine issue as to any material fact and that the moving party is entitled to a judgment as a matter of law." MRCP 56(c). Appellate courts apply a de novo standard in reviewing the grant or denial of summary judgment motions, making its own determinations separate and apart from the trial court. Lowery v. Guaranty Bank and Trust Co., 592 So.2d 79, 81 (Miss.1991). On a motion for summary judgment, a court does not try issues of fact; it can only determine whether there are issues to be tried. Hartford Cas. Ins. Co. v. Halliburton Co., 826 So.2d 1206, 1209-10(6) (Miss.2001) (citing Brown v. Credit Ctr., Inc., 444 So.2d 358, 362 (Miss.1983)).

8. For a plaintiff to recover in a slip-and-fall case, he must show one of the following: (1) a negligent act by the defendant caused the plaintiff's injury; (2) the defendant had actual knowledge of a dangerous condition; or (3) a dangerous condition existed for a sufficient amount of time to establish constructive knowledge of a dangerous condition. Munford, Inc. v. Fleming, 597 So.2d 1282, 1284 (Miss.1992).

A) Whether Gold Strike Caused a Dangerous Condition

9. Mississippi law requires the owner or operator of a business to "exercise reasonable care to keep the premises in a reasonably safe condition." Jerry Lee's Grocery, Inc. v. Thompson, 528 So.2d 293, 295 (Miss.1988). No proof of the owner's knowledge of the condition is necessary where the condition is created by his negligence or the negligence of someone under his authority. Drennan v. Kroger Co., 672 So.2d 1168, 1171 (Miss.1996). No one disputes that the placement of the plants, the maintenance of the plants, and the maintenance of the floors are all within the control and authority of Gold Strike.

10. To prove that Gold Strike maintained its premises in a reasonably safe condition, Gold Strike's guest service manager testified as to the procedures in place to maintain the lobby area of the hotel. He explained that the hotel hires two internal maintenance employees who are responsible for policing the

floor for spills and debris. These employees walk the entire lobby floor at least twice an hour. They are hired for the specific purpose of insuring that there is no debris, no stains, and no spills. These employees inspect the entire floor space in the lobby to make sure that there are no spills or stains. In addition, each employee, regardless of their job duties, is responsible for cleaning or reporting any stains, spills, or debris

[908 So.2d 774]

left on the floor. The guest services manager ensures that the employees are doing their job by personally inspecting the premises. He requires that the internal maintenance manager perform the same duty.

11. Even though the procedures Gold Strike uses to maintain its lobby are adequate to keep the premises in a safe condition, these procedures do not necessarily establish that the lobby was in a reasonably safe condition on the day of the accident. On the day of the accident, no one could testify as to the last time Gold Strike's employees inspected the lobby. While all Gold Strike employees were supposed to clean spills, these employees may have breached that duty. The guest services manager was not working at the casino on the day of the fall. He had no personal knowledge of whether or not the internal maintenance employees actually performed the inspections. For this reason, a question of fact exists for the jury whether the presence of water on the floor violated Gold Strike's duty to keep its premises in a reasonably safe condition. The bellman noticed that the individuals who water the plants carry towels with them to clean up spills. This fact puts the employees on notice that the area where the plants are watered is particularly susceptible to spills.

12. Gold Strike argues that it is speculative at best to claim that the water Mrs. Elston slipped on came from the plants watered by the agents of Gold Strike. Hundreds of guests walk through the lobby each day, and Gold Strike argues that it is pure speculation that the Elstons can trace the slip-and-fall accident to a condition that Gold Strike created. We disagree with Gold Strike that the Elstons merely speculated that the water she slipped on came from the plants. No one disputes that the substance she slipped on was water, the same substance that is used to wet the plants. It is therefore unlikely that the source of the spill came from a casino guest. Mrs. Elston fell in the immediate vicinity of the plants. The casino could not identify any other possible source of water other than from the plants. The plants are normally watered on Thursdays,

and Mrs. Elston's accident occurred on a Thursday.1 We find this evidence to be beyond speculation and sufficient for a jury to conclude that Mrs. Elston's injury was caused by a dangerous condition that Gold Strike created.

B) Whether Gold Strike Had Knowledge of A Dangerous Condition

13. Gold Strike did not possess actual knowledge of a condition that caused Mrs. Elston to slip and fall. Therefore, the Elstons wish to prove their case through constructive knowledge, showing that Gold Strike should have known that there was water on the floor. To establish a negligence claim under a constructive knowledge theory, proof of the water's presence on the floor for a sufficient period of time is required. Douglas v. Great Atlantic & Pac. Tea Co., 405 So.2d 107, 111 (Miss.1981). In Douglas, the supreme court affirmed the jury's verdict in favor of the defendant because "there was not a scintilla of evidence a third party created the wet hazardous condition; moreover, there was no proof the proprietor created the wet condition." Id. at 110. In Waller v. Dixieland Food Stores, Inc., 492 So.2d 283, 286 (Miss.1986), the supreme court affirmed the trial court's decision to grant a judgment notwithstanding the verdict

[908 So.2d 775]

because no evidence was produced tending to show how long the liquid was on the floor when the plaintiff slipped on it.

14. Both the Elstons and Gold Strike attempted to determine how long the water had been on the floor, but they were unable to do so. Unlike the facts in Douglas and Waller, however, the Elstons have presented more than a scintilla of evidence showing that the water had been on the floor for at least a few hours. Mrs. Elston's fall occurred on a Thursday, between 1:45 p.m. and 2:45 p.m. The plants were usually watered on Thursday some time between 10:00 a.m. and 11:00 a.m. This evidence can allow a jury to reasonably infer that the water had been on the floor for a sufficient period of time to establish that Gold Strike should have known the water was on the floor.

15. Gold Strike contends that the claim that the plants are watered only on Thursdays is speculative at best, because Magsby testified in his deposition that he merely "thinks" the plants are watered on Thursdays. We disagree. On the date of the deposition, Magsby had been an employee of Gold Strike

for three and a half years and had been employed as a bellman the entire time. During Magsby's shift, when he is not assisting customers checking into the hotel, he spends his time either behind the front desk or standing in the lobby waiting for patrons. During the time period of Mrs. Elston's fall, Magsby customarily worked every day from 6:00 a.m. to 2:00 p.m. The plants are located approximately ten feet from the front desk. On this evidence, a jury could find that Magsby observed the agents of Gold Strike water the plants on many occasions both before and after Mrs. Elston fell and had the credibility to assert that the plants are watered every Thursday morning. Even though Magsby was unable to state that he was absolutely certain that the plants were watered every Thursday, the Elstons have presented enough proof to allow a reasonable jury to decide whether the water came from the plants and was present on the floor for a long enough time to establish that Gold Strike had constructive notice of a dangerous condition.

16. Negligence of the defendant and notice to him may be found from circumstantial evidence of adequate probative value. Stated differently, "the plaintiff may prove circumstances from which the jury might conclude reasonably that the condition of the floor was one which was traceable to the proprietor's own act or omission." Winn-Dixie Supermarkets v. Hughes, 247 Miss. 575, 585, 156 So.2d 734, 736 (1963). In Hughes, the store manager was in the aisle where the slip-and-fall accident occurred three to five minutes before the plaintiff fell. He said he saw no foreign objects on the floor when he was there. Yet the store manager admitted that when he went to assist Hughes after she fell, the vermicelli upon which Hughes fell was on the floor and flowing almost to the check-out stand. Like the case sub judice, the store had in place a policy requiring all employees to be alert for objects on the floor. Id. at 737. Despite the manager's testimony that he saw nothing on the floor immediately prior to the accident and the store's policy that should have prevented the accident, the vermicelli was present when the plaintiff slipped and fell. Under the evidence, the trial court was allowed to submit to the jury the issue of liability on two theories: (1) the floor condition was traceable to the proprietor's own act or (2) that the store had constructive notice of the dangerous condition, because the store manager should have seen it. Id. Like Hughes, the case sub judice presents a factual question of causation that is subject to different determinations. K-Mart Corp. v. Hardy,

[908 So.2d 776]

ALISON PETERSON V. GROCERY DEPOT, INC.

735 So.2d 975, 983(20) (Miss.1999). These factual questions should be resolved by a jury.

17. Like the store manager in Hughes, Gold Strike's employees had ample time to observe the water on the floor, and no Gold Strike employee observed any spill on the day of the accident. The Elstons' assertion that the water had been on the floor for a sufficient length of time is supported by competent evidence. The Elstons have presented evidence showing that Gold Strike should have seen the puddle of water even if the water had been on the floor for a short period of time. The employees who investigated the accident after the fall estimated that the water was about five inches in diameter. Mr. Elston was able to see the puddle of water after Mrs. Elston fell. Mr. Elston testified that the back of Mrs. Elston's clothes was covered in water when she fell. He estimated that there was about half of a cup of water on the floor, and the puddle was deep enough that a person could feel the water if he put his hand in it. When Magsby, an agent of Gold Strike, was walking beside Mrs. Elston, he came within close proximity of the water, creating a jury question as to whether he should have seen the water upon which Mrs. Elston slipped. Morrison v. St. Luke's Health Corp., 929 S.W.2d 898, 903-04 (Mo.Ct.App.1996).2 This evidence is adequate to allow a jury to consider whether Gold Strike had constructive notice of the puddle in which Mrs. Elston fell.

CONCLUSION

18. To survive a summary judgment in a slip-and-fall case, a plaintiff must show that the defendant created an unreasonably dangerous condition, or he must show that the defendant had actual or constructive knowledge of a dangerous condition. On the evidence the Elstons have presented, a jury may conclude that Gold Strike was negligent, because it created a dangerous condition, and/or because it had constructive notice of the puddle of water upon which Mrs. Elston fell. Because we find that the Elstons presented enough evidence to show that there are genuine issues of material fact regarding the liability of the defendant, we reverse and remand to the circuit court.

19. THE JUDGMENT OF THE CIRCUIT COURT OF TUNICA COUNTY IS REVERSED AND REMANDED FOR PROCEEDINGS CONSISTENT WITH THIS OPINION. ALL COSTS OF THIS APPEAL ARE ASSESSED TO THE APPELLEES. KING, C.J., BRIDGES AND LEE, P.JJ., IRVING AND ISHEE, JJ., CONCUR. GRIFFIS, J., DISSENTS WITH A SEPARATE WRITTEN OPINION JOINED BY

MYERS AND BARNES, JJ.

GRIFFIS, J., dissenting:

20. I respectfully disagree with and dissent from the majority's finding.

21. The trial court correctly granted summary judgment because the Elstons did not establish a prima facie case against Gold Strike. The trial court found that there was not sufficient evidence of the source of the water. I agree. The only testimony is from Mrs. Elston that she

[908 So.2d 777]

"presumed" she slipped in water from the plants. Mrs. Elston's testimony is not based on her personal knowledge, and it is her speculation at best. The trial court also found no facts that would establish that Gold Strike caused a dangerous condition or that Gold Strike had either actual or constructive knowledge of any hazard. I agree with the learned trial judge.

22. A business owner owes a business invitee a duty of ordinary care to keep the business premises in a reasonably safe condition. Waller v. Dixieland Food Stores, Inc., 492 So.2d 283, 285 (Miss.1986). The owner has a duty to warn invitees of dangerous conditions which are not apparent to the invitee, of which the owner or occupier knows or through the exercise of reasonable care should know. Id. The owner is not an insurer against all injuries which may occur on the premises. Jerry Lee's Grocery, Inc. v. Thompson, 528 So.2d 293, 295 (Miss.1988).

23. In Munford, Inc. v. Fleming, 597 So.2d 1282, 1284 (Miss.1992), the supreme court established the standard by which a plaintiff may recover in a slip and fall case:

> [A plaintiff] must show the proprietor had actual knowledge of a dangerous condition, or the dangerous condition existed for a sufficient amount of time to establish constructive knowledge, in that the proprietor should have known of the condition, or the dangerous condition was created through a negligent act of a store's proprietor or his employees.

A plaintiff may proceed under any of the three alternatives. Nevertheless,

ALISON PETERSON V. GROCERY DEPOT, INC.

the plaintiff must offer some credible evidence to create a genuine issue of material fact in dispute about the defendant business owner's liability.

A. Whether Gold Strike caused a dangerous condition.

24. One theory of recovery, argued by the Elstons, is that the water was present due to the negligence of Gold Strike. "When the dangerous condition is traceable to the proprietor's own negligence, no knowledge of its existence need be shown." Waller, 492 So.2d at 285. However, in Sears, Roebuck & Co. v. Tisdale, 185 So.2d 916, 917 (Miss.1966), the court held:

> [P]roof merely of the occurrence of a fall on a floor within business premises is insufficient to show negligence on the part of the proprietor. Proof that the floor on which the fall occurred had present thereon litter and debris is similarly insufficient; and the doctrine of res ipsa loquitur is inapplicable in cases of this kind.

25. A question of fact does not exist simply because water was on the floor. The Elstons offered no credible evidence to establish that Gold Strike caused the water to be on the floor. The testimony of a doorman that he "thinks" the plants are usually watered on Thursday between 10:00 and 11:00 a.m. (the accident occurred between 1:45 and 2:45 p.m.) certainly cannot be characterized as direct or conclusive evidence that the water came from the plants. The doorman admitted that he did not see the plants watered the day Mrs. Elston fell. Mrs. Elston testified that she "presumed" the water came from the plants. The Elstons' response to the motion for summary judgment included the excerpts of several depositions, and no one testified that the water came from the plants.

26. The majority recognizes that "hundreds" of guests walk through the Gold Strike lobby every day. It is just as plausible, yet speculative, that one of the guests spilled water they were carrying as it is that water leaked from the plants. Mrs. Elston's and the doorman's testimony is indeed speculative. The jury's role is to consider the relevant and credible facts

[908 So.2d 778]

and then decide the case based on the law. It is a search for truth. The jury may not hold a defendant liable and award damages based on speculation

STATE OF FOSTER STATUTES AND CASES

alone. The evidence presented here indicates that there are no genuine issues of a material fact in dispute and that Gold Strike is entitled to a judgment as a matter of law that it did not cause a dangerous condition (i.e. the water) to be on the floor of the lobby.

B. Whether Gold Strike had knowledge of a dangerous condition.

27. If the presence of a dangerous condition is due to the act of a third party, the plaintiff must show that the defendant had actual or constructive notice of the hazard. Douglas v. Great Atl. & Pac. Tea Co., 405 So.2d 107, 110 (Miss.1981); Millers of Jackson, Meadowbrook Road, Inc. v. Newell, 341 So.2d 101, 102 (Miss.1977). The majority agrees that there is no evidence that Gold Strike had any actual knowledge that water was present in its lobby. The Elstons presented no proof in the record that any employee of Gold Strike knew that the water was present. Gold Strike's Guest Services Manager testified that Gold Strike employees periodically walked the premises, including the lobby, to inspect the floor and report any spills. If any were found, they would have the spills cleaned up. Thus, the only theory upon which the Elstons could rely is whether Gold Strike had constructive knowledge of a dangerous condition which caused Mrs. Elston to slip and fall.

28. To rely on the doctrine of constructive notice, the plaintiff must establish that the dangerous condition existed for such a length of time that the defendant, in the exercise of reasonable care, should have known of it. Douglas, 405 So.2d at 110. Here again, there is simply no evidence to support a finding of constructive notice. The majority determines that there is "more than a scintilla of evidence showing that the water had been on the floor at least a few hours." I disagree.

29. The doorman testified that he "thinks" the plants were watered on Thursdays, and they will water the plants between 10:00 and 11:00 a.m. He did not testify that he saw the plants being watered that morning. He did not even testify that watering the plants usually or ever causes puddles of water on the lobby floor. Instead, he stated that the individual who waters the plants also has a towel to clean up any spills.

30. The majority has taken this testimony of what is possible or might have happened (the plants may have been watered between 10:00 and 11:00 a.m.) and pieces it with what did happen (Mrs. Elston fell between 1:45 and 2:30

ALISON PETERSON V. GROCERY DEPOT, INC.

p.m.) to conclude that a jury could infer that the water had been on the floor a sufficient time to provide Gold Strike notice of its existence. This is conjecture and speculation. Accepting the testimony in the record, it is equally plausible that the jury could conclude that another patron spilled water immediately before Mrs. Elston fell. The question is not what the jury could infer but whether there any credible evidence to support the jury's decision.

31. The majority attempts to distinguish Douglas and Waller, but relies on Mississippi Winn-Dixie Supermarkets v. Hughes, 156 So.2d 734, 736 (Miss.1963) and Morrison v. St. Luke's Health Corp., 929 S.W.2d 898, 903-04 (Mo.Ct.App.1996). I disagree with the majority's analysis of these cases and application of legal principles.

32. In Douglas, Ms. Douglas went to the A & P for groceries. Douglas, 405 So.2d at 108. She was standing near the frozen food case with a basket full of groceries when she slipped and fell on something

[908 So.2d 779]

wet. Id. After she fell, the store manager saw "about a gallon or so of water on the floor adjacent to the frozen food case. He did not know how long the water had been there, but was sure it came from the frozen food case." Id. The store manager also testified that his accident report stated that the water on the floor was caused by the "frozen food case leaking water on the floor." Id. He further testified that the floor was cleaned approximately six hours before the accident, and he regularly walks the aisles each day. Id. The morning of Ms. Douglas' fall, he stated that he walked the store about six to eight times. Id. His last trip down that aisle was about and hour and a half before Ms. Douglas fell. Id. at 108-09. Before Ms. Douglas' fall, the frozen food case had not leaked. Id. at 109.

> 33. The supreme court concluded:
> Here there was not a scintilla of evidence a third party created the wet hazardous condition; moreover, there was no proof the proprietor created the wet condition. Thus it was the plaintiff's burden to prove either actual or constructive notice on the part of the proprietor of the dangerous wet condition of the floor in front of the frozen food case....
> It is possible to reasonably infer from circumstantial evidence

STATE OF FOSTER STATUTES AND CASES

presented at trial that the water originated from the adjacent frozen food case; however, even if this be so, proof of the water's presence on the floor for a sufficient amount of time to give reasonable notice to the proprietor is required. This the appellant did not prove. A similar case to the present is Hill v. Allied Supermarkets, Inc., 42 N.C.App. 442, 257 S.E.2d 68 (1979) where plaintiff slipped and fell on some water next to a vegetable bin in a supermarket. There was no evidence to indicate the source of the water or how long the water had been there, and plaintiff's testimony that she guessed the water came from the vegetable bin was viewed by the North Carolina Court as speculation and conjecture. In affirming the directed verdict for the proprietor, that court reasoned as follows:

Moreover, even if the speculations of the plaintiff and her witness identifying the bin as the source of the water should turn out to be correct, there is no evidence as to how long the water had been there nor was there any evidence to show that the defendant knew or in the exercise of reasonable inspection should have known of its presence in time to have removed it before plaintiff stepped into it and fell. There was no evidence that the freezing components of the vegetable bin were malfunctioning in any way or that, if they were, defendant knew or in the exercise of reasonable inspection should have known that this was the case. The testimony of plaintiff's niece that the water "maybe dripped" and that "(w)hen something is defrosting, the more it defrosts or runs the more water," obviously represents no more than speculation on her part. Such conjectures as to possibilities furnish no adequate basis for a jury finding that water in fact did drip from the vegetable bin as result of defrosting and that the dripping water did accumulate on the floor over a long enough period of time to give defendant notice of its presence. Upon all of the evidence, the jury could do no more than speculate about the water's source and about the length of time it had been on the floor. 257 S.E.2d at 71.

While it is quite true the frozen food case was under the superior control of the A & P, we recognize the well settled

[908 So.2d 780]

rule which disallows the application of the doctrine of res ipsa loquitur to slip and fall cases.

Douglas, 405 So.2d at 110-11. [citations omitted.]

34. Just as in Douglas, the testimony of neither Mrs. Elston nor the doorman is sufficient to furnish an adequate basis for the jury to find that Gold Strike caused the presence of the water or occurred over a long enough period to give Gold Strike notice of its presence.

35. In Waller, the supreme court determined that the evidence was insufficient to support a jury verdict. Waller, 492 So.2d at 286-87. Mr. Waller slipped and fell at the Piggly Wiggly Supermarket of Taylorsville. Id. at 284. He testified that "he slipped in a puddle of pink liquid he estimated to be eight to ten inches in diameter." Id. The store manager testified that he waxed the floors early that morning but did not use a pink liquid. Id. at 285. He also testified that he and his assistants regularly walked the aisles and he last walked the aisles at 10:00 a.m. Id. The accident happened at 12:30 p.m. Id. The jury awarded Mr. Waller $44,100, and the trial judge granted a judgment notwithstanding the verdict. Id. The trial judge found:

> In this case there is no evidence as to what the object or substance was or how it got there. There is also no evidence as to how long the object or substance had been on the floor. The only evidence as to whether or not the defendant knew that the object or substance was on the floor was testimony offered by the defendant that he did not know that the object or substance was on the floor.
> Id. The supreme court agreed and held:
> Did the manager have actual notice of the spill or did the spill exist for such a length of time that the manager should have known of it through the exercise of reasonable care?
> There was no evidence at trial that Phillip Skinner or any of his employees knew of the spilled liquid. To the contrary, Phillip Skinner testified that nothing regarding the spilled liquid had been brought to the store's attention before the allegations

STATE OF FOSTER STATUTES AND CASES

made by Mr. Waller. Additionally, there was no evidence tending to prove how long the pink liquid had been on the floor when Mr. Waller slipped in it. To establish a negligence claim in a slip and fall case, proof that the liquid's presence on the floor for a sufficient amount of time to give reasonable notice to the proprietor is required. Douglas v. Great Atlantic & Pacific Tea Co., 405 So.2d at 111.

The only time frame established during the trial was that Phillip Skinner personally inspected the aisles at 10:00 a.m. and that Mr. Waller slipped in aisle three at 12:30 p.m. If the evidence is taken in the light most favorable to the appellant, there was a two and one-half hour lapse between the last documented inspection by Mr. Skinner and the fall of Mr. Waller. Is proof of a two and one-half hour time lapse sufficient to prove how long the liquid had been in the aisle? This Court holds that it is not.

A similar question was addressed by this Court in Aultman v. Delchamps, 202 So.2d 922 (Miss.1967). In Aultman, the appellant unsuccessfully relied on the presumption that the store had opened at 8:00 a.m. and that the object she slipped on at 9:30 a.m. had been on the floor of the store for one and one-half hours. The Court responded:

It does not follow that because the store opened at eight o'clock that at precisely that time some person threw the dark object on the floor. It is just logical to assume that the object was

[908 So.2d 781]

thrown there two or three minutes before she stepped on it, and such a presumption is not sufficient to sustain a recovery on the theory that the object had been placed there and remained there for a sufficient length of time so that the appellee by the exercise of reasonable care should have known of the dangerous condition and removed the object from the floor.

Aultman v. Delchamps, 202 So.2d at 924.

Likewise, in the present case, it is just as logical to presume the liquid was spilled at 12:29 p.m. as it is to presume the liquid was spilled at 10:01 a.m. The former presumption is even more credible in light of Phillip Skinner's testimony that the liquid did not appear smeared and it did not appear as if anyone had pushed a buggy through it. Therefore, this Court does not believe the time lapse was sufficient to prove the length of time the liquid had been in the floor.

Waller, 492 So.2d at 286 (Emphasis added).

36. Thus, the supreme court has held that lapse of two and one-half hours was insufficient standing alone to prove how long a puddle of pink liquid had been on the floor. Id. The dangerous condition could have occurred at the beginning of the time frame or just before the plaintiff came into contact with the condition. Id.; see also Aultman, 202 So.2d at 924 (not logical to assume that a dangerous condition occurred at the beginning, rather than the end, of a given time frame). Thus, the court held that the trial judge correctly granted a judgment notwithstanding the verdict because the only way that a jury could have found against the defendant would be "through unreasonable speculation." Waller, 492 So.2d at 286.

37. Just as in Waller, Mrs. Elston's testimony that she "presumed" the water came from the plants and the doorman's testimony that the plants are usually watered on Thursdays between 10:00 and 11:00 a.m. does not furnish an adequate basis for the jury to find that the water had been on the floor for a long enough period to give Gold Strike notice of its presence.

38. In Hughes, Mrs. Hughes slipped and fell "on some dry vermicelli (edible paste smaller than spaghetti)." Hughes, 156 So.2d at 735. The jury awarded her $40,000, and the supreme court affirmed. Id. Mrs. Hughes went to look for rice when she slipped on some vermicelli that had fell on the floor from a damaged package on the shelf. Id. at 737. The store manager testified that the package of vermicelli was on the floor but other evidence indicated that the package was on the shelf after her fall. Id. A witness testified that the package "looked as if `it either had been cut by a case opener or gouged by a long finger nail.' His `judgment' was `that it was cut.'" Id.

39. The trial court reviewed the evidence based on the theory that Winn-Dixie caused the dangerous condition or had constructive notice. Id. First, the supreme court determined that there was a reasonable basis for the jury to trace the dangerous condition to Winn-Dixie's own act. Id. The court concluded

STATE OF FOSTER STATUTES AND CASES

that the evidence allowed a reasonable inference that "the damaged package of vermicelli was cut by the case-opening knife, when the original container was opened, and was placed on the shelf in that condition." Id. Thus, the jury could have determined that the package was cut by a Winn-Dixie employee then placed on the shelf. Id.

40. Next, the court determined that the jury could have reasonably concluded that "the vermicelli was on the floor at the time [the store manager] Glass was checking

[908 So.2d 782]

the stock in that aisle about five minutes before the fall, and he simply overlooked it, and the damaged package was either on the shelf or floor at that time; that in the exercise of reasonable diligence, Glass should have seen it, recognized the danger it presented, and should have removed it." Id. Thus, the jury could reasonably infer that the store manager was negligent in not observing the vermicelli on the floor when he was on the aisle moments before. Id. at 737-38. Also, the court considered testimony from a cashier who stated that, at approximately the same time as the fall, she then saw some children walk "past the check stand with loose `spaghetti' in their hands." Id. at 738. From this evidence, the jury could have determined that this was sufficient notice of the dangerous condition and the cashier was negligent by not "investigating further the source of the `spaghetti' and determining whether any more of it was on the floor, and in not notifying other employees of these facts." Id. The supreme court found that there was evidence to support liability under either theory, actual cause or constructive notice. Id.

41. In this case, there was no similar testimony. No individual could testify where the water came from. The claim that it came from watering the nearby plant is a guess, speculative at best. In Hughes, there was credible evidence to support the jury's finding that Winn-Dixie either cut the package before it was placed on the shelf, the store manager overlooked the spilled vermicelli when he walked the aisle moments before Mrs. Hughes fell, or the cashier was negligent when she learned that there may have been a spill. Id. at 737-38. Such credible evidence is simply not present here.

42. The majority also cites Morrison v. St. Luke's Health Corp., 929 S.W.2d 898 (Mo.App.E.D.1996), but declines to adopt its ruling as controlling precedent. In Morrison, a medical clinic was charged with knowledge of a dangerous

condition where a patient, who was being escorted by a medical assistant, fell over an unattended briefcase in the hallway. Id. at 904. The majority cites this case for the proposition that the fact that Gold Strike's doorman had the opportunity to see the puddle of water just before the accident is a factor that the jury should consider to determine whether Gold Strike had notice of the existence of the water. Morrison is simply not the law in Mississippi.

43. Ms. Morrison was a ninety-two year old woman with vision problems and osteoarthritis. Id. at 900. She fell over the unattended briefcase when she was being guided from the waiting room to the examining room by a medical assistant. Id. at 901. There is certainly a difference between a medical assistant escorting a blind and crippled elderly patient during a visit to her physician and a doorman assisting a healthy patron through a casino lobby. Here, there is no evidence that Mrs. Elston was elderly, vision impaired or needed assistance walking through the lobby. The fact that the doorman was walking beside her is not enough to establish that Gold Strike was or should have been aware of the existence of the puddle of water.

44. The evidence presented here indicates that there are no genuine issues of a material fact in dispute and that Gold Strike is entitled to a judgment as a matter of law that it did not have actual or constructive knowledge of a dangerous condition which caused Mrs. Elston to slip and fall. For these reasons, I dissent.

MYERS AND BARNES, JJ., JOIN THIS SEPARATE WRITTEN OPINION.

Notes:
1. Gold Strike argues that it is mere speculation that the plants were watered on Thursday. We disagree with this assertion and address this issue in a later part of this opinion.
2. This Court recognizes that Morrison is not binding precedent, and we decline to adopt a per se rule holding that an agent who escorts another individual through a dangerous condition is on notice of an unreasonably dangerous condition. Nevertheless, the fact that Magsby had the opportunity to see the puddle of water immediately prior to the accident is a factor the jury can consider in deciding whether Gold Strike should have seen the puddle of water.

STATE OF FOSTER STATUTES AND CASES

ALISON PETERSON V. GROCERY DEPOT, INC.

BRIEF OF SULLIVAN V. SKATE ZONE, INC.
FACTS OF THE CASE
These are the most basic facts that make up this case that must be known to determine an outcome.

ISSUE
What is the main concern in this case that the court is faced with resolving?

RULE OF LAW
What statues and case law are used to help determine the outcome of this case.

ANALYSIS
This combines the facts with the issue as applied to the rules of law. Be careful to pull this apart one element at a time.

CONCLUSION
This is a simple statement of which party won

STATE OF FOSTER STATUTES AND CASES

Summary of the points in this case that you can use to either support your case or plan a defense.

FIRST STEP
Number every paragraph in the case. Even if the paragraph is only one sentence, number it so you may make a reference to it if needed.

SECOND STEP
In the margin write "Test" if the court is applying a test. If there are multiple parts to the test, mark the elements as follows, "T-1, T-2, T-3, ..." If there is more than one Test in the case, mark the second Test and elements as follows, "Test-2, T2-1, T2-2, T2-3, ..."

THIRD STEP
In the margin mark the final Holding of the case with "Held" and underline the key phrases.

FOURTH STEP
List the parts of this case that you will need to work with to support or plan a defense for your case. Use the paragraph numbers and test numbers you have just finished putting on the case itself for referencing back to the case.

List your case parts, phrases and references below:
1.

2.

3.

4.

5.

6.

7.

STATE OF FOSTER STATUTES AND CASES

SUPPORTING INFORMATION

ALISON PETERSON V. GROCERY DEPOT, INC.

EVIDENCE SUBJECT TREE

PRELIMINARY MATTERS

SCOPE
All matters are subject to the breadth of the issue being defined

Judicial Notice
Allows the Judge to accept into evidence general knowledge that is readily determinable

Burden of Proof Civil Actions
Preponderance of the evidence. Basically the 51% rule.

Burden of Proof Criminal Actions
Beyond a reasonable doubt. Often referred to as the 99% rule but there is no actual standard supporting this belief.

PROBATIVE SUFFICIENCY

RELEVANT EVIDENCE
Includes: Logical, Accurate portrayal, Scientific, Similar Happenings, other legal matters dealing with character

PREJUDICE, CONFUSION, OR WASTE OF TIME
Evidence may be excluded based upon any of these reasons

HABIT
These are personal traits that have a high degree of regularity

EVIDENCE SUBJECT TREE

PROBATIVE SUFFICIENCY Continued

OPINION

EXPERTS
Experts must qualify with the following test: Have special knowledge, training, skills, education or experience within the field of expertise. Experts may speak to the ultimate issue with an opinion

LAY PERSON
Must have personal knowledge that is relevant and within the scope. Cannot speak or give an opinion on the ultimate issue

PROBATIVE SUFFICIENCY of PRIVILEGES

ATTORNEY / CLIENT
Client is holder of the privilege and attorney must remain loyal

DOCTOR / PATIENT
Patient is holder of the privilege and doctor must remain loyal

HUSBAND / WIFE
Both are holders of the privilege and must remain loyal even after divorce for matters during the marriage

ALISON PETERSON V. GROCERY DEPOT, INC.

EVIDENCE SUBJECT TREE

WITNESS RELIABILITY

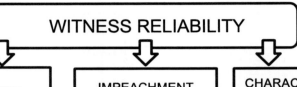

MEMORY
Attorney may refresh witness' memory with leading questions, but the witness cannot read from notes

IMPEACHMENT
May establish this through personal bias, character reputation, prior bad acts, felony convictions, prior inconsistent statements

CHARACTER
May establish reputation in the community, known opinions, and specific actions

RELIABILITY
Evidence may be considered reliable if any one of the following may be established (MIMIC): Motive, Intent, Absence of Mistake, Prior Identification, and Common Plan or Scheme

HEARSAY

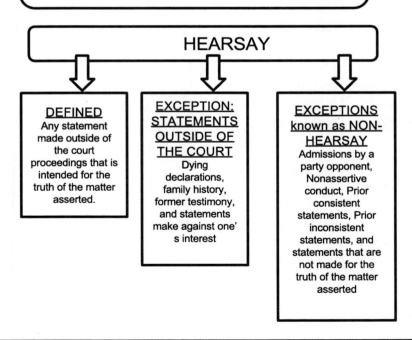

DEFINED
Any statement made outside of the court proceedings that is intended for the truth of the matter asserted.

EXCEPTION: STATEMENTS OUTSIDE OF THE COURT
Dying declarations, family history, former testimony, and statements make against one's interest

EXCEPTIONS known as NON-HEARSAY
Admissions by a party opponent, Nonassertive conduct, Prior consistent statements, Prior inconsistent statements, and statements that are not made for the truth of the matter asserted

SUPPORTING INFORMATION

ALISON PETERSON V. GROCERY DEPOT, INC.

EVIDENCE LAW OUTLINE

1. PRELIMINARY MATTERS
1.1. Scope
1.1.1. These rules govern all proceedings both civil and criminal
1.1.2. Exceptions to these rules:
  1.1.2.1. Preliminary questions of fact
  1.1.2.2. Grand jury proceedings
  1.1.2.3. Extradition proceedings
  1.1.2.4. Preliminary examination in criminal cases
  1.1.2.5. Sentencing phase of the trial in a criminal case
  1.1.2.6. Issuance of warrants for arrest
  1.1.2.7. Search warrants

1.2. Burdens and Presumptions
1.2.1. Civil Actions
  1.2.1.1. Preponderance of the evidence is the general standard of persuasion. Commonly known as the 51% rule.
  1.2.1.2. Clear and convincing evidence. This may be used in cases involving fraud or the validity of a testamentary document.
  1.2.1.3. Judicial notice. This is when the judge accepts the evidence as admissible due to generally known knowledge or it is readily determinable.
1.2.2. Criminal Actions
  1.2.2.1. Beyond a reasonable doubt. Commonly referred to as the 99% rule but that is in error since there is no real percentage standard to what a jury may consider beyond a reasonable doubt.
  1.2.2.2. Judicial Notice. This is when the judge accepts the evidence as admissible due to generally known knowledge or it is readily determinable.

2. PROBATIVE SUFFICIENCY
2.1. Relevant Evidence
2.1.1. Relevant evidence is that which has the tendency to make the existence of any fact more or less probable.
2.1.2. Logical
  2.1.2.1. Foundation. Must offer sufficient evidence to establish a finding that the evidence is what it is claimed to be.
    2.1.2.1.1. Public records. If the public record is certified as a public record, it is self authenticating

2.1.2.1.2. Photograph. Not always self evident.

2.1.3. Lay person. May testify if the person is familiar with the topic prior to litigation.

2.1.4. Expert witness. May testify to the the details of the topic he/she has knowledge. May give an opinion that is solely based upon his/her expertise.

2.1.5. Similar happenings or Lack of similar happenings. Must be established prior to the event at trial.

2.1.5.1. May show bias or prejudice

2.1.5.2. May show undue delay

2.1.5.3. May show obstruction of investigation

2.1.6. Prejudice, Confusion, or Waste of Time. Evidence may be excluded for any one of these reasons:

2.1.6.1. Prejudicial. The probative value is substantially outweighed by the danger of unfair prejudice.

2.1.6.2. Confusion. The probative value is substantially outweighed by the danger of confusion of the issues.

2.1.6.3. Waste of Time. The probative value is substantially outweighed by the danger of wasting the courts time due to needless presentation of cumulative evidence.

2.1.7. Habit. Personal traits that are done with a high degree of regularity. May establish the following:

2.1.7.1. Conduct in conformity with other actions being charged, or not in conformity.

2.1.7.2. No specific eye witness is necessary.

3. PRIVILEGES
3.1. Foundational Test for All Privileges
3.1.1. Does a protected relationship exist?

3.1.2. Does a confidential communication exist?

3.1.3. Has the holder of the privilege waived the privilege?

3.1.4. Is there an exception to the privileged communication?

3.2. Attorney / Client
3.2.1. Client is the holder of the privilege. Attorney must be licensed in at least one state. Exceptions include:

3.2.1.1. Suits between client and Attorney

3.2.1.2. Suits among joint clients

3.2.1.3. Future crimes that are admitted and planned by client

3.3. Doctor / Patient
   3.3.1. Patient is the holder of the privilege. Doctor must be licensed to practice. This privilege protects medical diagnosis information and treatment based upon that diagnosis. Exceptions include:
   3.3.1.1. When the physical condition of the patient itself is the issue at trial, the privilege is waived.
   3.3.1.2. Criminal proceedings in general for information that leads to a crime and gives information about it.
   3.3.1.3. Malpractice actions that are brought by the patient.
   3.3.1.4. Competency proceedings that challenge the competency of either the doctor or patient.

3.4. Psychotherapist / Patient
   3.4.1. Patient is the holder of the privilege. Psychotherapist must usually must be licensed but some states allow for marriage and social counselors to be bound under this privilege. Exceptions include:
   3.4.1.1. No privilege when mental condition is at issue.

3.5. Husband / Wife
   3.5.1. Both are holders of the privilege and either can assert the right even after the marriage is dissolved for matters that occurred during the marriage. Includes confidential communication between husband and wife. Exceptions include:
   3.5.1.1. Crimes against the spouse or children
   3.5.1.2. Statements made in furtherance of a future crime or fraud.
   3.5.1.3. Actions that are witnessed by the spouse.

4. RELIABILITY
4.1. Witnesses. To be a witness one must:
   4.1.1. Take an Oath to tell the truth
   4.1.2. Have mental Capacity
   4.1.3. Possess knowledge of the matter at issue
   4.1.4. The judge and jurors may not testify

4.2. Memory. Each witness must have the ability to recall from memory the events at issue. However, the memory is allowed to be refreshed under the doctrine of Refreshed Recollection as follows:
   4.2.1. Leading questions are allowed to refresh memory
   4.2.2. Witness may use notes but cannot read from notes
   4.2.3. Opposing counsel has the right to inspect the notes and documents from the witness

4.3. Impeachment

4.3.1. Intrinsic Impeachment. This is testimony from the mouth of the witness, which is established to be untrue.

4.3.2. Extrinsic Impeachment. All other evidence not from the mouth of the witness that established the testimony to be untrue.

4.3.3. Methods of Impeachment

    4.3.3.1. Bias in the issue at bar includes:

        4.3.3.1.1. Interest in the outcome

        4.3.3.1.2. Relationship

        4.3.3.1.3. Hostility

        4.3.3.1.4. Fee paid to an expert

    4.3.3.2. Character of the Witness

        4.3.3.2.1. Reputation. This includes opinions that are known

        4.3.3.2.2. Bad acts that are non-convictions but well-known that relate to honesty

        4.3.3.2.3. Felony convictions

        4.3.3.2.4. Convictions of crimes involving dishonesty and morality include misdemeanors.

        4.3.3.2.5. Prior inconsistent statements made by the witness

        4.3.3.2.6. Sensory defects This establishes a credibility problem and impeachment may result.

4.3.4. Character

    4.3.4.1. Foundation test:

        4.3.4.1.1. Determine the form of the evidence

        4.3.4.1.2. Determine the type of case: civil or criminal

        4.3.4.1.3. What purpose the evidence will be used

    4.3.4.2. Form test:

        4.3.4.2.1. Reputation. This will establish the reputation of the person in the community

        4.3.4.2.2. Opinions of the person's character are allowed if the witness has personal knowledge

        4.3.4.2.3. Specific good and bad acts may be testified to

    4.3.4.3. Civil Cases

        4.3.4.3.1. Character evidence is inadmissible to prove the conduct at issue is in conformity with prior actions

        4.3.4.3.2. Exceptions:

            4.3.4.3.2.1. If character is an essential element as in cases like defamation and child custody

            4.3.4.3.2.2. Knowledge and care of another person is at issue

4.3.4.3.2.3. Self defense
4.3.4.3.2.4. Negligent entrustment
4.3.4.4. Criminal Cases
4.3.4.4.1. Defendant may use circumstantial character evidence in three ways;
4.3.4.4.1.1. Opening the door rule. Evidence of good character is allowed by the reputation and opinion to establish innocence for the particular charge/crime.
4.3.4.4.1.1.1. Prosecution may rebut with reputation and opinion evidence.
4.3.4.4.1.2. Bad Character of Victims. Reputation, opinion and specific acts are all admissible.
4.3.4.4.1.3. Rape cases. Reputation and opinion evidence is inadmissible. Specific acts of sexual acts are admissible if:
4.3.4.4.1.3.1. Behavior that explains signs of rape
4.3.4.4.1.3.2. Past behavior with defendant establishing consent
4.3.5. MIMIC. Evidence is most generally admissible if used to show:
4.3.5.1. Motive
4.3.5.2. Intent
4.3.5.3. Mistake. Lack of making a mistake
4.3.5.4. Identification
4.3.5.5. Common Scheme or Plan that has been used by defendant in the past
4.3.6. Best Evidence Doctrine. The Best Evidence applies if:
4.3.6.1. Original document must be used and produced when:
4.3.6.1.1. Words of the document has independent legal significance
4.3.6.1.2. The testimony of the witness is reliant upon the document and not upon the personal knowledge

4.4. Opinion Testimony
4.4.1. Expert Opinion
4.4.1.1. Qualifying Test:
4.4.1.1.1. Expert must have special knowledge, training, skills, education, or experience
4.4.1.1.2. Opinion must be helpful to the fact finder
4.4.1.1.3. Opinion must be within field of expertise

4.4.1.2. Basis of Opinion for Experts:
    4.4.1.2.1. Facts perceived or made known at or before time of trial
    4.4.1.2.2. need not have personal knowledge of the issue at trial
    4.4.1.2.3. Expert may make an opinion of the ultimate issue before the court
4.4.2. Lay Person Opinion.
    4.4.2.1. Must have personal knowledge
    4.4.2.2. Must be rationally based upon the perception of the witness
    4.4.2.3. Must be helpful to the fact finder
    4.4.2.4. Must be relevant

5. HEARSAY
5.1. **Defined:** Hearsay is a statement that was made out of court that is now repeated in court to prove the truth of the matter asserted.
5.2. **Exceptions: Unavailability of Witness Required**
    5.2.1. Unavailability must be due to one of the following:
        5.2.1.1. Absence from the court's jurisdiction
        5.2.1.2. Assertion of a privilege
        5.2.1.3. Declarant is dead
        5.2.1.4. Lack of memory
        5.2.1.5. Refusal to testify
    5.2.2. Dying Declaration
        5.2.2.1. Statement must have been made with the belief that death was imminent, but actual death is not required
    5.2.3. Family History
        5.2.3.1. Family history that is known from a variety of sources
    5.2.4. Former Testimony
        5.2.4.1. Must have been given in an earlier proceeding with the same opposing party
    5.2.5. Statements made against the person that has now caused him/her to be unavailable
5.3. **Exceptions: Availability of Witness is Immaterial**
    5.3.1. Ancient documents. Must be more than 20 years old
    5.3.2. Business Records. Records or reports kept in the regular course of business.
        5.3.3. Catch-All. Evidence that is more probative than any other

evidence and the evidence cannot be admitted under another exception.

5.3.4. Documents relating to property interest.

5.3.5. Excited Utterance. Statements made while under the stress of excitement.

5.3.6. Family Records. Family bibles, engravings on tombstones, inscriptions on family portraits, etc.

5.3.7. Learned Treatise

    5.3.7.1. Must be found to be authoritative by an expert testimony

    5.3.7.2. Must be called to the expert's attention

    5.3.7.3. Treatise is merely read into evidence and comes in for the truth of the matter asserted

5.3.8. Market reports for value and other conditions

5.3.9. Physical condition and mental state of the person

5.3.10. Present sense impressions. This is the immediate sense of the person at the time.

5.3.11. Prior convictions. Must be a final judgement and is admitted for the truth of the matter asserted.

5.3.12. Public reports.

5.3.13. Records of vital statistics including birth, death marriage, etc...

5.4. Exceptions: Non-Hearsay

5.4.1. Admission by a Party Opponent (APO). Statements made by either party may be quoted by others.

5.4.2. Prior Consistent and Inconsistent Statements are all admissible.

SUPPORTING INFORMATION

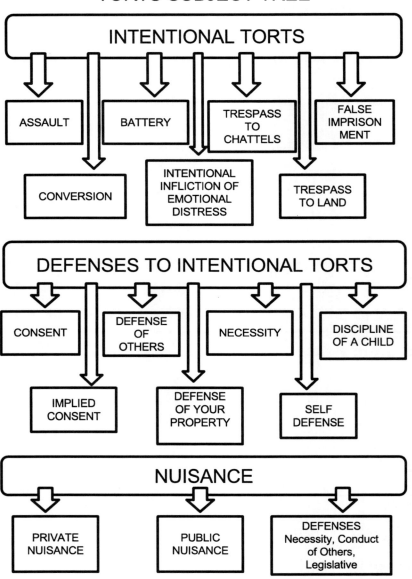

SUPPORTING INFORMATION

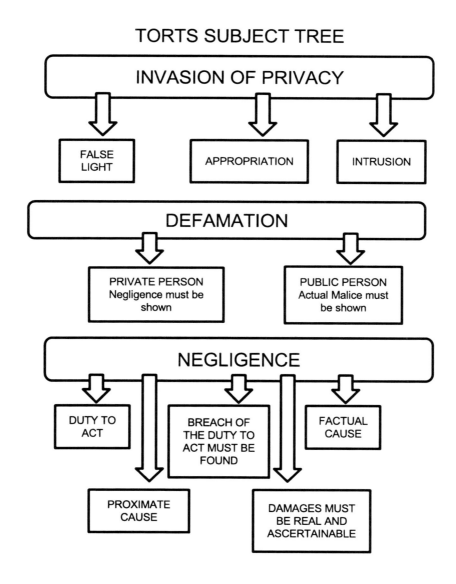

TORTS LAW OUTLINE

1. INTENTIONAL TORTS
1.1. Definitions
1.1.1. General Intent. The person did not necessarily intend to cause the harm, but the person is the one responsible for the harm.
1.1.2. Specific Intent. The person planned to do the action that either directly caused the harm or put the ultimate object into play that caused the harm.
1.1.3. Transferred Intent. Harm intended against person A but harmes person B thereby allowing intent to transfer to a third party.
1.1.4. Reasonable Prudent Person (RPP). This is a standard of care applying to all persons declaring that we must all act with at least as much care as a reasonable prudent person.
1.2. Assault
1.2.1. Defendant must intend to put the plaintiff in imminent apprehension of harmful or offensive contact.
   1.2.1.1. Plaintiff need not be in fear of the assault
   1.2.1.2. Plaintiff must be aware of the threat giving rise to the assault
   1.2.1.3. Threats declared upon an unascertainable date are not actionable
   1.2.1.4. Harsh words alone are not enough to create an assault
1.3. Battery
1.3.1. Intentional harmful or offensive contact of the person.
   1.3.1.1. Anything the person is holding, touching, sitting in or on is an extension of the person.
1.4. Conversion
1.4.1. Interference with chattel so great it takes the full value. This is a permanent taking or destruction of the item.
1.5. Trespass to Chattels
1.5.1. Slight interference with plaintiff's possession of the chattel.
1.5.2. Slight dominion or control over plaintiff's chatel is enough
1.6. False Imprisonment
1.6.1. Defendant intends to confine plaintiff
   1.6.1.1. Confinement must result within a fixed boundary
   1.6.1.2. Threat of force may result in confinement
   1.6.1.3. Physically holding a person is confinement
   1.6.1.4. Any amount of time or duration is actionable

SUPPORTING INFORMATION

    1.6.1.5. There cannot be any reasonable means of escape
    1.6.1.6. Plaintiff must be aware of confinement
1.7. Intentional Infliction of Emotional Distress
    1.7.1. The conduct must be extreme, outrageous, and exceed all boundaries of decency.
        1.7.1.1. Physical injury is not required
        1.7.1.2. A third party may recover if:
            1.7.1.2.1. The plaintiff is a family member of the harmed person
                1.7.1.2.1.1. Defendant must be aware of the third person
    1.7.2. Types of mental suffering that may be actionable:
        1.7.2.1. Anger
        1.7.2.2. Disappointment
        1.7.2.3. Embarrassment
        1.7.2.4. Fright
        1.7.2.5. Grief
        1.7.2.6. Horror
        1.7.2.7. Humiliation
        1.7.2.8. Nausea
        1.7.2.9. Shame
        1.7.2.10. Worry
1.8. Trespass to Land
    1.8.1. Physical invasion of real property by the person or causing an object to enter another's property.
    1.8.2. It is enough that the person intended to be on the property whether he/she realized the it was a trespass or not.
    1.8.3. Sleepwalking does not equal trespass to the land because the person must consciously intend to be there.
    1.8.4. Runaway horse or automobile does not equal trespass to the land because the person must consciously intend to be there.
    1.8.5. Under or above the property may be trespass
    1.8.6. Smoke and Gasses drifting on the property is a trespass

2. DEFENSES TO INTENTIONAL TORTS
2.1. Consent
    2.1.1. Actual consent may be oral or written
    2.1.2. Consent must be voluntary
    2.1.3. Person must have mental capacity to consent
    2.1.4. Mistake, Duress, or Fraud may negate consent

2.2. Trespass to Chattels
- 2.2.1. If the person's chattel is on another's property:
  - 2.2.1.1. Person must make a demand to recover the chattel
  - 2.2.1.2. Reasonable force is allowed to enter another's property to recover the chattel.

2.3. Defense of Others
- 2.3.1. Person must have reasonable belief that the person being harmed is in need of a defense

2.4. Defense of Property
- 2.4.1. Only reasonable force is allowed
- 2.4.2. Cannot ever use deadly force to recover property

2.5. Implied Consent
- 2.5.1. Person must have capacity
- 2.5.2. Implied consent may arise from custom
- 2.5.3. Implied consent may arise from usage
- 2.5.4. May be implied by emergence conditions.

2.6. Discipline
- 2.6.1. Parents have an absolute right to discipline their children
- 2.6.2. Discipline must be reasonable
- 2.6.3. Teachers of children may use reasonable force to restrain and discipline

2.7. Necessity
- 2.7.1. Private necessity to trespass. No liability for trespass but person is liable for damages
- 2.7.2. Public necessity to trespass. No liability for trespass and no liability for damages

2.8. Self Defense
- 2.8.1. Person must have honest believe he/she is in need of defense
- 2.8.2. Only reasonable force is allowed
- 2.8.3. Deadly force is allowed if threatened with deadly force
- 2.8.4. There is no duty to retreat

3. NUISANCE
- 3.1. Threshold Tests
  - 3.1.1. Private Nuisance
    - 3.1.1.1. Plaintiff must have suffered some type of actual harm or injury to his/her property. Harm must be:
      - 3.1.1.1.1. Substantial, and
      - 3.1.1.1.2. Unreasonable, and

SUPPORTING INFORMATION

    3.1.1.1.3. Interferes with another's use and enjoyment of the property
   3.1.2. Public Nuisance
    3.1.2.1. The public has suffered a harm causing the danger of:
     3.1.2.1.1. Public health
     3.1.2.1.2. Public peace
     3.1.2.1.3. Public safety
3.2. Defenses to Nuisance
 3.2.1. The conduct of others gave rise to this situation
 3.2.2. Contributory negligence
 3.2.3. Legislative authority gave rise to act
 3.2.4. Necessity

4. DEFAMATION
4.1. Elements
 4.1.1. Must be a living person
 4.1.2. The defamatory language must affect the person's reputation
 4.1.3. Language must be of and concerning the person
 4.1.4. Statements giving rise to the harm must be published to a third person
 4.1.5. Damages for Defamation may be presumed for all the following:
  4.1.5.1. Person is declared to have a loathsome disease
  4.1.5.2. Woman is declared to be unchaste
  4.1.5.3. Person is declared to have committed improper professional conduct
  4.1.5.4. Person is falsely accused of a moral crime
 4.1.6. Private person must show the conduct by another was Negligent
 4.1.7. Public person must show the conduct by another person was done with Actual Malice
4.2. Defenses to Defamation
 4.2.1. Truth is a complete defense. if the defendant can prove the statements were true, that is a complete defense.
 4.2.2. Consent by the plaintiff to use these statements
 4.2.3. Retraction is not a defense
 4.2.4. Absolute privileges:
  4.2.4.1. Judicial proceedings
  4.2.4.2. Legislative proceedings
  4.2.4.3. Executive proceedings
 4.2.5. Qualified privileges
  4.2.5.1. Public interest may rise to a level for a need to know

5. INVASION OF PRIVACY
5.1. False Light
5.1.1. Plaintiff has been subjected to an objectionable use of his/her character - usually a moral character issue. Must be objectionable to a reasonable prudent person under the circumstances.
5.2. Appropriation
5.2.1. Unauthorized use of plaintiff's picture or name for commercial use or gain.
5.3. Intrusion
5.3.1. Prying or intruding that is objectionable to a reasonable prudent person.
5.4. Private Facts
5.4.1. Public disclosure of private facts. The publication must be:
- 5.4.1.1. Objectionable to a reasonable prudent person, and
- 5.4.1.2. Must not serve a legitimate public interest.

6. NEGLIGENCE
6.1. Prima Facie Case
6.1.1. Duty of care, and
6.1.2. Breach of the duty of care, and
6.1.3. Causation, and
- 6.1.3.1. Actual causation, and
- 6.1.3.2. Proximate causation

6.1.4. Damages
6.2. Duty of Care
6.2.1. There are many different duties of care that may apply according to the class of person involved. Commonly thought of as "Class of Person - Class of Risk." Major duties of care include the following:
- 6.2.1.1. Reasonable Prudent Person. All physical handicaps are considered and the plaintiff is expected to act with the disability.
- 6.2.1.2. Automobile passengers. This class of persons are treated as licensees; therefore, the driver must warn passengers of known defects.
- 6.2.1.3. Children. Held to a standard of care of other children of like age and skills.
- 6.2.1.4. Insanity and mental incompetents. No differences are made for mental conditions.
- 6.2.1.5. Professionals. Must use the skills of a professional in the area.

SUPPORTING INFORMATION

6.2.1.6. Relationships. Family members must give aid, rescue and give assistance to the level of his/her ability.

6.2.1.7. Trespassers.

    6.2.1.7.1. Undiscovered trespassers are owed no duty of care.

    6.2.1.7.2. Discovered trespassers. Discovered includes anticipated trespassers:

    6.2.1.7.3. Must warn of concealed, unsafe, artificial conditions that are known.

    6.2.1.7.4. No duty to warn of natural conditions.

6.2.1.8. Infants

    6.2.1.8.1. Attractive nuisance will apply if:

    6.2.1.8.1.1. Artificial dangerous condition is on the land

    6.2.1.8.1.2. Child fails to appreciate the danger because of age

    6.2.1.8.1.3. Expense of repairing danger is slight in comparison with the risk

    6.2.1.8.1.4. Owner knew or should have known children are in the vicinity.

6.2.1.9. Licensees

    6.2.1.9.1. These people are invited or have permission to enter the land/building. These are usually called social guests. There is no duty to inspect or warn of dangerous conditions.

6.2.1.10. Invitees

    6.2.1.10.1. This class of persons includes businesses and land open to the public.

        6.2.1.10.1.1. There is a duty to inspect, and

        6.2.1.10.1.2. Duty to make safe.

6.3. Breach of the Duty of Care

6.3.1. Breach occurs when the defendant has not performed up to the stated standard of care that is owed to the plaintiff. Some special areas for breach of the duty of care include:

    6.3.1.1. Res Ipsa Loquitur

    6.3.1.2. Negligence Per Se

    6.3.1.3. Common Usage doctrine

6.4. Causation. Both parts of causation must be proven.

6.4.1. Actual Causation (Factual Causation) the test is as follows:

    6.4.1.1. But for the event the plaintiff would not have been harmed. The actual cause must have been a substantial factor of the harm.

6.4.2. Proximate Causation (legal causation)

6.4.2.1. The harm to the plaintiff was foreseeable by the reasonable prudent person and the event was either the direct or indirect cause of the harm.

6.5. Defenses to Negligence

6.5.1. Assumption of the risk. No recovery for damages at common law if the following are proven:

6.5.1.1. Plaintiff voluntarily subjected herself to the risk, and

6.5.1.2. Plaintiff willingly subjected herself to the risk, and

6.5.1.3. Plaintiff knowingly subjected herself to the risk.

6.5.2. Contributory negligence. No recovery of damages at common law.

6.5.2.1. If plaintiff is found to have contributed in any manner or amounts, plaintiff is unable to recover damages.

6.5.3. Comparative fault. (several states such as Oregon use this standard for the defense allowed). This defense comes in two types:

6.5.3.1. Pure comparative fault. Plaintiff's damages are reduced by the amount of fault due to plaintiff. Even if plaintiff is found to be more than 50% at fault, this does not stop recovery of damages. For example, if plaintiff is found to be 70% at fault, plaintiff may still recover 30% of damages from defendant. (several states such as Oregon use this standard)

6.5.3.2. Traditional comparative fault. If plaintiff's fault is at least 50% or greater, no recovery of damages.

6.6. Negligent Infliction of Emotional Distress

6.6.1. Defendant must demonstrate a threat of physical or emotional impact occurred and resulted in actual physical symptoms

6.6.1.1. Defendant must be found to have created the risk, and

6.6.1.2. Defendant's conduct caused tangible physical injury, and

6.6.1.3. Plaintiff must have been within the zone of danger.

7. STRICT LIABILITY

7.1. Products. Selling a product in a defective condition and/or unreasonably dangerous condition to the user may be held strictly liable for all damages.

7.1.1. Disclaimers do not overt strict liability

7.1.2. Failure to provide adequate warning may result in strict liability

7.1.3. The only defense to strict liability is assumption of the risk.

7.2. Ultra Hazardous Activities. Strict liability applies whenever an abnormally dangerous activity is involved. Two part test:

7.2.1. There must be a risk of serious harm, and

7.2.2. Activity is one not commonly engaged in.
7.3. Wild Animals. The wild animal does not have to possess the ability to harm the plaintiff. Rather, it is enough that the animal is in the class of wild animals and the injury is the type that would be expected by the animal

7.3.1. Wild animals cannot ever be domesticated no matter how tame it appears.

8. OTHER TORT LIABILITIES
8.1. Vicarious Liability
8.1.1. Respondeat Superior. Employer is liable for the acts of his agents and employees.

8.1.1.1. Act must be done within the scope of employment

8.2. Parents Liability of their Children
8.2.1. Parents are not liable for the tortious acts of their children

8.2.2. Parents are possibly liable for the negligent acts of their children if there is failure to supervise and control their children.

ALISON PETERSON V. GROCERY DEPOT, INC.

SUPPORTING INFORMATION

BRIEFING A LEGAL CASE
Understanding how to brief a legal case is an important skill. This skill will allow you to find the critical facts, issue, rule of law, and the conclusion while stripping the excess information away from the case. Good briefing allows you to quickly look through the cases and find the pertinent information without delay as well as concisely be on-point with the issue you are grappling. Be careful to not be biased. Biases can destroy an otherwise good analysis.

The following procedure is referred to as the IRAC method, which is very popular and works very efficiently when used to its fullest potential, so let's walk through it. First, let's get a basic story to help us work through this.

John and Taylor were at a baseball park, and each were coaching young baseball teams. An argument broke out concerning whether John's player had struck out or if it was another foul ball. As the two stood there about ten feet apart, John swung a bat back and forth while stating in an angry rage "I hate you Taylor. You always try to get away with stuff like this. Someday you will pay for this." Taylor spat on the ground in front of John and said, "Idiot! You are making something out of nothing." Tempers flared as both men walked back to the dugout. While on the way back to the dugout, Taylor turned around and threw a rock at John and hit him in the leg, but John did not feel it.

FACTS – always start with finding the core facts to the case. These facts are the established facts of the case that are not in contest. It is important to realize what facts are not in dispute and which ones are being argued. Example facts may be as follows:
- John and Taylor were at a baseball park.
- Each was the coach of a young baseball team.
- John and Taylor were about ten feet apart. John swung a bat back and forth.
- John stated, "I hate you Taylor. You always try to get away with stuff like this. Someday you will pay for this."
- Taylor said, "Idiot! You are making something out of nothing."
- While on the way back to the dugout, Taylor turned around and threw a rock at John and hit him in the leg, but John did not feel it.

ISSUE – the issue is likely the most important element to get right from the beginning because it is driving the remainder of the briefing. The issue should be stated as concisely as possible, but try to use language that is not tied so directly to your specific case that the issue cannot be used in another case.

ALISON PETERSON V. GROCERY DEPOT, INC.

For example:
- Difficult to use again – Whether John committed the tort of assault when he swung the bat at Taylor.

- This may be improved as follows – Whether the tort of assault may be established when an object is swung at another person.

RULE – the rule is simply the law on-point. This part is usually fairly easy to find as it can normally be found in the jurisdiction's statutes. There also may be rules that are common usages in the area. An example of a rule is as follows:

Under the law of assault the following elements must be established: Imminent
- Imminet
- Apprehension
- Harmful
- Touching
- Of another person
- Specific intent

These do not have to be in a bulleted list, and many rules of law will not neatly fit into such a list.

ANALYSIS – now this is when you get to really show off your skills. The analysis part is where it all comes together. Combine the core facts, rule (one piece at a time. E.g. Imminent, Apprehension, ...), and the issue to argue that each element is established (or not established as the case may be against you). It is imperative that you take your time and argue one step at a time. Let's go through an example of how this may work.

- Here we see that John was holding a baseball bat in his right hand swinging the bat back and forth, and John was standing about ten feet from Taylor. We are told that John has used threatening words; "I hate you Taylor" and, "Someday you will pay for this." Looking to our first two elements of imminent and apprehension it is unclear that Taylor was put in a place of harm being imminent because the threat was for the future – "Someday." Concerning the apprehension element, John was standing ten feet away from Taylor, but with the reach of John's arms plus the length of the bat it may be possible that Taylor was in apprehension of being hit. It is unclear if he was apprehending being hit because of threat or just misuse of swinging the bat.

SUPPORTING INFORMATION

- Here, you would continue the analysis walking through all the elements.

CONCLUSION – the conclusion is to be a simple statement as a natural outpouring of the analysis. Do not continue to argue the case here. If you have further arguments, you need to go back to the analysis part. Let's look at an example:

- Therefore, the tort of assault may not be established because the elements of Imminent and Apprehension could not be conclusively shown.

ALISON PETERSON V. GROCERY DEPOT, INC.

MOTION IN LIMINE

A motion in limine is a pretrial motion that is made to request the court from hearing evidence that is highly prejudicial to the moving party during the trial. The burden is upon the moving party to show that curative instructions to the jury will not prevent a prejudicial effect upon the jury. The motion is written as follows:

1. Specific identification of prejudicial evidence.
2. Issue: state the issue that the evidence is concerning.
3. Rule/law: is there a specific rule on point as to why this evidence should not come in during the trial? If not, move to analysis next.
4. Analysis: fully explain why this evidence is so damaging and prejudicial that a jury would be unduly influenced by this piece of evidence and distracted from the issue(s) being tried in the court.
5. Conclusion: make your final statement asking for elimination of this evidence from the trial.

SUPPORTING INFORMATION

RHYTHM OF A TRIAL

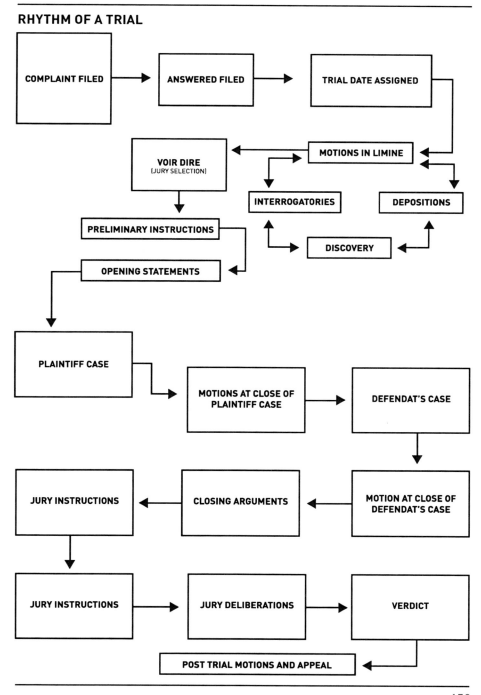

ALISON PETERSON V. GROCERY DEPOT, INC.

LIST OF COMMON OBJECTIONS

AMBIGUOUS
Confusing, misleading, vague

ARGUMENTATIVE
The question makes an argument rather than asking a question.

ASKED AND ANSWERED
When the same attorney continues to ask the same question.

ASSUMES FACTS NOT IN EVIDENCE
The facts being testified to have not been entered into evidence.

BADGERING
Antagonizing the witness in order to provoke a response.

BEST EVIDENCE RULE
Requires that the original source of evidence is required, if available.

BEYOND THE SCOPE
A question asked during cross-examination has to be within the scope of direct examination.

CALLS FOR A CONCLUSION
The question asks for the witness to form an opinion that creates a conclusion for the jury to accept.

CALLS FOR SPECULATION
The question asks the witness to guess the answer rather than to rely on known facts.

COMPOUND QUESTION
Multiple questions asked together.

COUNSEL IS TESTIFYING
Question is not really a question; rather, the question is testimony from counsel.

SUPPORTING INFORMATION

HEARSAY
The witness does not know the answer personally but heard it from another. There are many exceptions to the rule of Hearsay.

INCOMPETENT
The witness is not qualified to answer the question.

INFLAMMATORY
The question is intended to cause prejudice.

IRRELEVANT OR IMMATERIAL
The question is not about the issues in the trial.

LEADING QUESTION
Generally not permitted on Direct Examination, but is permitted on cross-examination.

MISSTATES EVIDENCE
Improper characterization of the evidence.

NARRATIVE
The question asks the witness to relate a story rather than state specific facts.

RELEVANCE
Question is not relevant to the matter before the court.

ALISON PETERSON V. GROCERY DEPOT, INC.

SUPPORTING INFORMATION

ALISON PETERSON V. GROCERY DEPOT, INC.

GLOSSARY

AFFIRMATIVE DEFENSE
An affirmative defense to civil lawsuit is a fact or set of facts other than those alleged by the plaintiff and if established by the defendant, defeats or mitigates the legal consequences of the defendant's unlawful conduct.

ADMISSION BY A PARTY OPPONENT (APO)
This serves as one of the large exceptions to the Hearsay rule. Generally, if a person is on the witness stand in court and is quoting another person's statements, that is usually hearsay. However, if the person being quoted is one of the listed parties in the lawsuit action itself (does not include witnesses to the lawsuit) other parties may quote statements from these parties and it will not be considered hearsay.

ANSWER
The pleading filed by the defendant in a civil action in response to the complaint, which is a formal written statement that admits or denies the allegations in the complaint and sets forth any available affirmative defenses.

CIRCUMSTANTIAL EVIDENCE
Evidence that is not based on actual personal knowledge or direct observation of the facts in contest. Instead, this evidence is based upon supporting facts that allow for personal inference, which support an actual basis in fact without having personal knowledge of the initial evidence.

COMPLAINT
The Pleading that initiates a civil action

CROSS-EXAMINATION
This is an examination of the witness by the opposing party. All questioning must be within the scope of the Direct Examination testimony. Questions are usually closed ended resulting in short and concise answers to stay within the scope of Direct Examination.

DAMAGES
An award, usually money, to be paid to a person as compensation for loss or injury.

DEFENDANT
The person defending or denying; the party against whom relief or recovery is sought in an action or suit, or the accused in a criminal case. In every legal

GLOSSARY

action, whether civil or criminal, there are two sides. The person suing is the plaintiff and the person against whom the suit is brought is the defendant. In some instances, there may be more than one plaintiff or defendant.

DEPOSITION
An out-of-court oral testimony of a witness that is reduced to writing for use in a court or for discovery purposes.

DIRECT EVIDENCE
Evidence that is based on actual personal knowledge or direct observation of the facts in contest.

DIRECT EXAMINATION
The first examination of a witness on the merits by the party that the witness is called to testify on behalf of. Direct examination usually sets the scope for future cross-examinations. Questions are usually open ended allowing the witness to tell the story.

HEARSAY
An out of court statement. Numerous rules of evidence for the hearsay doctrine are difficult to reduce into simple definitions. Generally, any quoting of statements made by another person may be considered as hearsay. Please see in this index Relevancy, Admission by a Party Opponent.

INTENTIONAL TORT
Category of torts that describes a civil wrong resulting from an intentional act on the part of the tortfeasor.

MOTION IN LIMINE
A motion in limine (Latin: "at the start", literally, "on the threshold") is a request to a judge that can be used for civil or criminal proceedings that is written and also in many cases argued orally to the judge. Motions In Limine pre-trial or during the trial to remove evidence from being heard as part of the case.

NEGLIGENCE
Conduct that falls below the standards of behavior established by law for the protection of others against unreasonable risk of harm. A person has acted negligently if he or she has departed from the conduct expected of a reasonably prudent person acting under similar circumstances.

ALISON PETERSON V. GROCERY DEPOT, INC.

OBJECTION
A motion made during a trial to stop the introduction of evidence by a witness or other forms. Most often objections are made orally during the court setting and may include having the jury removed during the discussion.

PLAINTIFF
The party who sues in a civil action. Also known as the complainant.

RELEVANCY
U.S. law is reflected in Rule 401 of the Federal Rules of Evidence, "having any tendency to make the existence of any fact that is of consequence to the determination of the action more probable or less probable than it would be without the evidence."

STARE DECISIS
Precedent or authority and is a principle or rule established in a previous that is either binding on or persuasive for a court when deciding subsequent cases with similar issues or facts.

TORT
A civil wrong, or wrongful act, whether intentional or accidental, from which injury occurs to another. Torts include all negligence cases as well as intentional wrongs which result in harm. Also known as Personal Injury Law.

TRIAL
A judicial examination and determination of facts and legal issues arising between parties to a civil or criminal action.

UNINTENTIONAL TORT
An injury caused without intent because one does not abide by the legally required standard of care. Most common form of unintentional tort is negligence.

GLOSSARY

ALISON PETERSON V. GROCERY DEPOT, INC.

CPSIA information can be obtained at www.ICGtesting.com
Printed in the USA
BVOW04s0439210314

348331BV00002B/11/P